# The Winds of God

HOWARD A. GOSS

Copyright © 2018 by Curry R. Blake

All Rights Reserved

Published by

Christian Reality Books

P.O. Box 742947

Dallas, TX 75374

This book or parts thereof may not be reproduced in any form without express written permission of Curry Blake.

Cover Design by Courtney Nelson

Printed in the United States of America.

# THE STORY OF THE EARLY PENTECOSTAL DAYS (1901-1914)

A CHRISTIAN REALITY BOOKS
PENTECOSTAL HISTORY CLASSIC
**REPRINT**

| | |
|---|---|
| Introduction | 6 |
| Chapter 1 | 8 |
| Chapter 2 | 15 |
| Chapter 3 | 20 |
| Chapter 4 | 24 |
| Chapter 5 | 28 |
| Chapter 6 | 34 |
| Chapter 7 | 38 |
| Chapter 9 | 48 |
| Chapter 10 | 56 |
| Chapter 12 | 72 |
| Chapter 13 | 75 |
| Chapter 14 | 88 |
| Chapter 15 | 99 |
| Chapter 16 | 105 |
| Chapter 17 | 111 |
| Chapter 18 | 117 |
| Chapter 19 | 121 |
| Chapter 20 | 135 |
| Chapter 21 | 142 |
| Chapter 22 | 146 |
| Chapter 23 | 154 |
| Chapter 24 | 162 |
| Chapter 25 | 176 |

*Chapter 26..............................................................................187*
*Chapter 27..............................................................................194*
*Chapter 28..............................................................................207*

# Introduction

After many years of studying Pentecostal history, I was blessed to come across a book by Howard Goss entitled: "The Winds of God". I can say without exaggeration that this book was instrumental in changing my life into what it is today.

I have read many books about the early days of the Pentecostal Outpouring, but only two books can be attributed with such drastic effect. One is the book you are now reading, and the other is the book entitled: "Azusa Street", written by Frank Bartleman.

After I had read this book, I found out that it was out of print and thus no longer available to this generation of Christians. I knew then that I would someday reprint it exactly as it was first released. This I have now done.

Once you read this book you will never be able to be the same. The level of commitment to the preaching of the gospel these people exhibited, shames all of us who have or are living the "normal" Christian life of a twentieth-century Christian. When you compare their "sold-out" Christian lives to our lives of "sold-out" Christianity", it will make you reassess your salvation.

Nothing else mattered to these people except making sure that every person heard the gospel and that their lives would faithfully represent the Christ they served.

As you read this book, I pray that you will get a vision of the type of Christianity that it was intended to perpetuate.

I have heard many people say that the level of zeal and commitment demonstrated here, is no longer necessary. But those that say such things have never come near equaling the fruit the early Pentecostals exhibited.

One thing that cannot be overlooked or overestimated is that these people lived this lifestyle and accomplished what they did. We do not live this lifestyle and we have not accomplished anywhere near what they did. They did all they did in a time that provided NO means of mass communication.

Yet rather than admit our folly and change our ways, we tend to make excuses and continue without results.

This one last thing I will ask you, when Jesus returns, will He find faith on the earth? Will He find it in you?

Rev. Curry R. Blake

# Chapter 1

Immediately after the Civil War my grandfather, Larkin Goss, moved from Tennessee and settled near Steelville, Missouri.

His son Clinton, with his Kentucky school teacher bride, Margaret Gillette, soon followed and homesteaded land near my grandfather's acreage, in 1883, on these three hundred twenty acres of virgin soil, only partially cleared, I was born.

In those days anyone who homesteaded land in Missouri could have all he needed. When my father and mother arrived, they settled amidst beautiful scenery and natural plenty. If the heavily wooded mountains and hills were covered with stones, the fertile valleys lay ready to feel the edge of the axe and-after much hard work-the bite of the plow.

They soon found that the forests around them abounded in wild game: turkey, deer, wild hogs, bears, opossums, wild fowl and small game-food for the experienced hunter as it came from the hot maw of his great wood-fired oven. Swift mountain streams teemed with fish. Forests of tall oak furnished the logs from which their two-storied houses and barns were constructed.

Into this boy's paradise seven sons were born, I being the fifth of the seven. Later two girls made it a family of nine children.

We were a hardy people, and the country matched us in hardships. There were no toys other than those we devised for ourselves. I used a large, old, discarded iron skillet, with a string tied through the handle, for a wagon.

Books we had but no shoes. They had to be handmade in our locality. Only the older boys had shoes bought for them. I was about twelve years old when I had my first pair, which was earlier than some of our neighbor boys acquired them.

We all worked from the peep of day until the darkness had settled down. Christmas Eve and the Fourth of July were our only holidays. On the "Fourth" we all attended a "Democrat" picnic, our only celebration in the entire year. On Christmas Eve we all drove to town to do our shopping.

Sunday afternoon was the only recreation time in the week. Then we boys were free to roam the hills, fields and woods for our own amusement. I early became an expert with the bow and arrow, and shot predatory birds in the trees and speared fish in the streams in this primitive Indian fashion. My older brothers had two guns for hunting, one a Winchester rifle and the other a muzzle-loading rifle. We had no feeling of lack, because our life seemed full to us and complete. Compared to those around us, it was. But we learned to work hard for everything we received. What we did have was plentiful enough, but money was very scarce. My father often sold a full wagon load of his finest Northern Spy apples for ten cents a barrel.

A few incidents will suffice; I think to depict my childhood days.

Teasing a large, vicious old bulldog was one of my main diversions. I would go up into the hay loft where the dog couldn't reach me, and throw hayseed down at him until he would be angry enough to tear me to pieces.

Sometimes he would come so near to catching me that, when I would dash across the yard in answer to the dinner horn, I would be forced to climb a tree for safety, and sometimes would have to remain there for hours.

My brother now claims it was my favorite way of escaping work. Usually my pockets were filled with seeds and clods, so that from the vantage point of a limb, I could still pelt the dog. It was always open warfare between us, as the farm work did not, by any means, use up all my energy. Many times the dog caught me and, aiming for my throat, would chew the arm with which I was protecting my throat, leaving the flesh hanging in ribbons. Being bit I would wait for a few days for the wounds to heal, and then would start teasing the dog again. Several of the worst scars show to this day.

While I was still quite young, my father sent me with a younger brother, Bryl, into a field to plant corn. On this particular day I had the hoe while Bryl carried a bag of shelled corn slung across his shoulder. We were to drop into the plowed furrow three or four grains of corn, push the loose dirt over them, tamp them down and move on to the next position. I became very weary and bored as the morning crawled by.

Starting to play a bit by way of distraction, we spilled the corn on the ground and then decided that it was too much work to pick up. Being two little boys alone in the field with a lot of unplanted

corn, we soon decided that the easiest way out would be the quickest way home. I dug a hole large enough to hold all the spilled corn and raked it in.

"And why not," I thought, "Father will never know." I carefully covered it over, tamped it down smoothly and felt relieved. Then we very soon forgot the whole incident.

But, alas, spring weather; the sun and the rain did their inevitable work. One Sunday, after Father had walked over his fields on a tour of inspection, he called me and returned with me to the corn field. There before my astonished and terrified gaze, the ground which I had left so smooth and flat was now bulging in a great mound, and from it a tangled mass of green, growing corn was shooting up. My father only pointed...without saying a word. But the punishment I received at the time taught me a life-long lesson, which I later learned was Biblically expressed in the words: "He that covereth his sins shall not prosper" and "Be sure your sins will find you out."

On Sundays my father usually sat in a great chair in the front porch when his weekly tour of inspection was over. At watermelon time he sat with an eagle eye watching the patch of melons in front of the house, guarding it from his young sons and their visiting friends. A stream which ran through the farm meandered through this particular field in a horseshoe shape; it was almost half a mile from the porch to the stream's farthest central curve. Through this field the water ran shallowly under deep, overhanging banks and over sandy bars.

Waiting for the melons to ripen was a long process, and we younger boys often became desperately impatient. One Sunday afternoon as father kept a sharp lookout for every leaf of twig that moved suspiciously, two or three other boys and I entered the stream bed well behind my father's line of vision. We came crouching, Indian-fashion, up the full length of the lazy creek bed, until we reached a point nearest the ripest melons.

Slithering carefully on our stomachs without disturbing so much as a leaf, we quietly edged our way over the field until each one of us had a melon detached from the vine. Rolling them carefully in front of us with our heads, we made our way back to the stream bed. We disappeared, each one of us triumphantly bearing a melon. All this had been done without arousing suspicion.

One of the visiting boys was a "softie" however. Later that afternoon, after we had eaten the green melons, we were in the blacksmith shop and two of the boys suddenly became sick. With no warning even to themselves, their rebellious stomachs scattered green watermelon seeds over the blacksmith shop floor.

I suffered painful consequences the next day after the blacksmith described the incident to my father.

Another pastime during the winter months was to see, every snowy morning, which boy in his bare feet could run around the house and back in the shortest possible time. We were full of pranks; we were healthy, hearty and young...and amused ourselves at every opportunity.

Once, according to Mother, us boys finally persuaded the "poor little girls," who were aged four and six, to run around the house barefoot in the snow. We solemnly promised them that if they would, we would show them the cutest pair of little white calves they had ever seen. To farm children, this was more than they could pass up. But they fled in shocked tears of disappointment to Mother when one of the boys only lifted the hem of their long skirts and showed them the calves of their own little white legs.

After almost forty years Mother's voice still betrayed annoyance and pity, as well as amusement, at the remembrance of our prankishness.

Ponds and streams of water, combined with the cold Missouri winters, afforded us plenty of opportunities for ice skating and I soon became very good at it. One winter the whole country was heavily covered with sleet. Our farm was on higher ground than the schoolhouse down in the valley which was about three and a half miles away. One day I decided to go across country to school on skates.

However, I wasn't yet experienced enough to allow for the down grade, so I quickly gained momentum I hadn't figured on. I shot down steep slopes, sailed over ice-covered stumps, jumped frozen streams and did all I could do to come out of my wild flight alive. But I still enjoyed skating.

Several years ago, I met an uncle, Jesse Goss, who was a postmaster for many years at West Plains, Missouri. Although retired, he still was active and in perfect health at eighty-seven years of age.

Talking reminiscently of our childhood days he said that after his return from the Spanish-American war, he came one day to visit my Father's family. Unexpected visitors soon arrived, and one of the older boys was sent out to cut some firewood for the kitchen stove. A younger brother tagged along, but Uncle Jesse had by this time forgotten which one. Standing on the back porch, Uncle Jesse said he could see the smaller boy playfully thrusting, between the axe blows, his bare foot onto the stick of wood he was cutting.

Finally, after repeated warnings, the child failed to remove his foot quickly enough and the axe severed the great toe from the foot. Only one slender cord of loose skin held the toe and foot together.

When Mother heard them call out, she hurriedly snatched the family wash basin, and pouring it full of cold water from the spring, went out to them, dashed both foot and toe into the cold water, placed them together again, bound them up, and hurried back into the house and resumed her dinner preparations.

Uncle Jesse said that was the last he ever heard of the incident. I had never heard of it, nor have any idea which one of us it was.

Nor do I ever remember having tasted medicine, nor having had any need for it, as I was never sick but once in my life and even then not for an entire day.

Once in a while some of us boys, as we grew older, would work at what was called "public work." This was in an iron furnace about three miles away. I was fourteen when I first went there, working with men who were filling the kiln with cordwood which was burned and made into charcoal for the furnaces. We worked twelve hours a day and were paid fifty cents a day. As this was very hard work, I naturally developed powerful muscles and consequently developed a strength that was far above the average.

# Chapter 2

In 1898 my father sold the farm and moved to Galena, Kansas, where a mining boom was surging in the lead and zinc mines. He invested in a mine which failed, and all our savings disappeared. Soon I secured a job in a mine where I replaced a man who had been killed the day before.

I soon became used to the "voices" of the mine-the rumblings of the earth-and got to understand their portent. In spite of this, I went into the mine one day just after the powder men had set off a blast and, without warning; a great pile of falling stone partly buried me. It cut my scalp in several places and knocked me unconscious. When I revived, I found myself lying on a couch in the company's office swathed on bandages. But I very soon was well enough to go back to work again.

Another accident occurred in the mines when another man and I fell down a mine shaft 125 feet deep. Waiting for the hoister to take us down. We had stepped onto the cage, of "bucket," before the operator arrived. The machinery slipped and down we shot. While I was falling, although I did not understand at the time why this should be, I saw all my sins depicted before me on the wall of that shaft.

Not believing in God, I could not connect this occurrence with Him. I did not even know I was a sinner, nor that I would have been eternally lost if I had died then.

When we struck bottom, the loading platform broke beneath us, and we plummeted into the sump water below. This saved our lives, after the platform had checked our fall. Nevertheless, I felt this came as a warning to me. I quit the underground work and went into the mining plant above ground.

Later I became a helper and was soon assistant to the overseer of the mill, and learned the trade of "steam jig" boss. When I was about nineteen, I was offered a great opportunity for advancement in the mining business, if I were to decide to make mining my life's work. I accepted, left the mines temporarily, and returned to high school to finish out the graduation year that was necessary to secure my promotion.

During the next few months of my school life in Galena many things happened. Physically, I was a natural athlete and fond of all sports. I tried a little of everything. Having previously done some boxing for the sake of exercise and, since I was light on my feet as well as fast, alert and strong, I soon gained quite a reputation in town, and developed quite a following.

Although I had not the least intention of boxing professionally, it seemed for a time that I could scarcely avoid such a future. But since I liked football much better I concentrated on that sport. I became captain of the high school eleven and later the captain of the professional team.

To keep in training I would run twelve miles every morning before breakfast. Of course I lived an abstemious life, a life of great self-control. I drank neither tea nor coffee, and I know now that football taught me many lessons which I probably could not have learned as easily in any other way.

I was able later in life to apply this knowledge to Christian work. My aim is still to see that the ball always reaches its goal; that God's side wins; that the devil is defeated and the organization they all have played their part in furthering God's kingdom.

The section of Galena in which I worked then was that of a typically wide-open, frontier mining boom-town, where everything went and where tent shacks abounded.

Rough men came from every direction, riding or driving through the deep mud or dust, whichever for the moment made up the newly laid-out streets. They drank, gambled, shot, fought or killed each other as they pleased. Largely making their own laws, they went their own ways, and worked in the mines when they felt like it, or when they ran out of money and were compelled to. In the business section almost every other building housed a saloon with brothels sandwiched in between.

Few were the mornings when I went to work that I did not see at least one dead man lying between the tent shacks where he had been thrown during the night to get him out of the way. After some nights there would be several bodies in evidence.

A railroad divided the town into two sections-like two armed camps. That is, insofar as the teenagers were concerned. When the boys from the "respectable" side of the tracks had to go on Saturday nights to draw their pay at the mine office, they rarely went alone. For safety's sake they usually went in gangs of twenty or so. Many interesting and wonderful fights were fought over nothing! But it was like fire to impetuous young blood and muscles, and we never tired of it.

Surprisingly enough, although we were surrounded by all this wickedness, we seven Goss boys remained respectable members of society and picked up practically none of the wicked habits of the men with whom we worked. Several of us began to use tobacco but only one ever took more than an occasional drink. Fortunately, we all grew up to become men of whom one could be proud.

None of us were Christians at the time. Far from it. We never had a Bible story told to us. We never read a Bible, attended a Sunday School, or a church in our lives. God was completely ignored in our home. Once my Mother told me that I could never be a truly educated man unless I had read at least some portions of the Bible. To please her I got a Bible and asked her where to read. She said anywhere she supposed. I opened at Matthew and after reading the first chapter through, I remarked:

"Well, if it is all like this, I do not want to read anymore of it."

She never mentioned it again. Consequently, I grew up quite free from the doubts, unbelief, and erroneous ideas which plague many a church member, I find, even today.

John, the third son in our family, was a staunch infidel all of his twenty-one years. Somewhere he had picked up some radical ideas. He read and passed on to us such authors as Paine, Voltaire, Ingersoll, and others. Some of us believed in infidelity, some of us were indifferent, but seemingly none of us saw any reason to refute it, so it became the accepted belief of some of us boys. As John was my ideal, I naturally became one of his strongest supporters. It had never occurred to me that we might all be wrong.

While he was on his deathbed he called me, who was his favorite, and admonished me to hold to infidelity, telling me that I was the wisest and most favored of all the children. He announced that someday I would make my mark in the world and have greater happiness than the others.

If this has been fulfilled at all, I feel that it was because I became the first in my family to find the Lord. When I did, I began regular attendance at all services. My soul's salvation and obedience to my new-found Savior was my goal.

# Chapter 3

My conversion from infidelity to Christ came about in this way. While attending high school in the late fall of 1902, Mrs. Mary Arthur, a devout Methodist, and her husband, who was the town's leading hardware merchant, invited Charles F. Parham, a former Methodist minister, to Galena to conduct evangelistic meetings. This evangelist erected a tent on the Arthur's front lawn and began preaching the new Apostolic (now Pentecostal) teaching.

Because of Charles Parham's revolutionary message, there was soon quite a stir. As he preached Divine Healing, many local people experienced God's healing for various of their diseases. Then Mrs. Arthur herself was healed of blindness which, due to her prominence in religious and social circles, attracted widespread attention.

Many other cases of blindness were healed. Cancers also disappeared. Multitudinous were the diseases and the ailments that were cured.

All these happenings were reported day after day at the high school where I was studying, since many of the students were attending the revival. Soon some of these same students said that they themselves were saved; a few even talked in a strange language and claimed that they were "baptized in the 'Holy Ghost'"- whatever that meant. Since they were boys and girls like the rest of us, I knew they understood no language other than their own. Curious, I too became interested.

This was my first contact with Pentecostal people... or with Christianity of any sort, for that matter. I was invited to go to the tent with some of the younger people.

After attending the service, it soon became evident to me that some superhuman power was at work there. Much to my surprise, I found myself beginning to be convinced that somewhere there existed a being whom men called God.

During the alter service one night I watched an old Indian chief receive the Baptism of the Holy Spirit. Tall and straight as an arrow, this old chief stood tilted rigidly backwards, yet maintained his upright position by balancing himself on the edge of his heels without any support. While he was raising God with uplifted hands, his body trembled rhythmically as if shaken by some great machine. This inflexible position he did not vary or relax in the slightest degree for over an hour. Then he began to speak in a strange language.

Unusually strong as I was, I knew that it was beyond ordinary human power to perform this feat, or many of the other things which I saw take place before my eyes. But this was the incident that finally capped my decision that there existed somewhere a Power higher than man. As I watched and cautiously listened further, I soon became fully convinced that there was a Supreme Being, and that His power was at work in our town.

Cold weather had driven the congregation from the tent into a large store building on Main Street which was called the Grand Leader Building. It must have seated 1000 people and out of the great crowds that attended, some 800 were converted and more than 1000 were truly healed, while many hundreds were baptized in the Holy Ghost as evidenced by their speaking in strange tongues according to Acts 2:4.

Miracles and wonders seemed to be a constant occurrence. I remember one young lady receiving the

Baptism of the Holy Ghost on Sunday night, and for seven days after to the hour she could not speak English. When the English language returned to her, it caused quite a stir and brought great conviction, for she was generally well known.

Ernest Hilliard's father, who had been seeking the Holy Ghost, awoke at four o'clock in the morning speaking in tongues, now he couldn't speak a word of English until the following Monday morning at exactly the same hour. He also was widely known, and these things truly became "a sign" and "a wonder" to the townspeople and to those in the vicinity.

I feel that I owe my conversion to Christianity to hearing people speak in other tongues. The 14th Chapter of 1 Corinthians tells us that "tongues are a sign to the unbelievers," and today I still thank God that I heard and saw His own sign from Heaven.

Around the time the Galena meeting first started, Mrs. Arthur's sister, who was also my high school teacher, detained me one day after school and spoke to me about serving the Lord. In all my life, this was the only time anyone had ever spoken to me about my soul. As can readily be imagined, I have always since been a firm believer in, and an advocate of Personal Evangelism.

After I became fully convinced that infidelity was wrong, I went forward during the next meeting to the place of prayer, earnestly praying and seeking God. I sought God every night for about two weeks and so far as I could tell no change of heart took place. But I persisted, for I had wholly given myself up to God and now wanted Christianity to be my entire way of life. Finally one night I physically felt my sins go from me and I knew within my heart that I was forgiven and pardoned.

I have often said publicly that once I became convinced that there was a God, then in order to be honest with myself and to do what was right, I had to serve Him. So, I thanked and praised God for what I, at long last, knew I had received from Him.

On one of the coldest days of the entire winter that followed, I can remember Brother Parham baptizing around 100 converts in the Spring River before a tremendous crowd assembled in the open. None of the converts who were baptized developed a cold as a result of their experience. I was one of that hundred.

# Chapter 4

The first Gospel preaching I had ever heard, needless to say, made a most profound impression upon me. I remember how attentively I listened that night.

This great Galena revival was the second ever to be held by Pentecostal people and took place in the fall of 1903. Brother Parham preached Jesus, His teachings, salvation, life, and the power to heal from Christ's time to the present moment.

He preached that when Jesus by death slipped out of His human body at Calvary, it did not lessen His power to heal, but rather increased it. The sufferings of Gethsemane and Calvary were all for us, in order that He might be "touched with the feeling of our infirmities." His power to heal after that was not through the natural man, the earthly Jesus, but was through His power, as the Son of God from Heaven.

Whenever there was a healing line, there would always be so many waiting to be prayed for that Brother Parham would sometimes become exhausted, and would have to finish praying for the remainder of the sick while sitting down. However, he seemed always fresh and strong for the next service.

He preached a clean holy life of victory for all believers, and the second work of grace as taught by Rev. A. B. Simpson. He emphasized the words and commands of Jesus and taught a clean separation from the old life. He seemed to "rejoice" in an opportunity to demonstrate Christ's teaching, such as "Give to every man that asketh of thee and from him that would borrow of thee, turn not away": "Overcome evil with good" and many other practical truths of the Word of

God. As he promised, obedience brought down upon us a "running over measure."

I assimilated all this as best I could, and when they told me I would now have to be sanctified as "a second definite work of grace," I went after this experience also, and soon received something which they said was "sanctification," a "dying out of the old man," and many other terms. I did not know what that I was now "a new creature" and full of the Lord, and that it was all most glorious.

God had surely changed my life. I was so happy that everything around me seemed fairly scintillating with joy. God had changed my whole outlook on life so completely that even the old mine dumps around Galena suddenly seemed beautiful.

Although I was interested in all kinds of sports, I now felt that God had a different work for me to do, and what little He allowed me to do, I did, whether I understood it or not.

I belonged to two secret lodge orders but I felt that they were not God's best for me, so I resigned from them as well as from the team. These and many other decisions I made for myself before hearing them mentioned from the pulpit. God somehow made plain to me what He wanted me to do and I did it. All my plans for the future were changed.

I was disconsolate over the time I had wasted reading newspapers. So, for two years after my conversion, I read nothing but my Bible and what a love I had for the word of God! Many nights I could not bear to lay it down even to sleep. I would lie all night long with the Bible folded in my arms upon my chest while I slept, so intense was my love for that blessed book. This exclusive reading of the Scriptures soon became a fixed habit. I would read it in every spare moment, even while at work when it was possible.

When I later temporarily returned to the "steam jig boss" work in the mine building where I was stationed, I found an old unused elevator shaft. It was small and without a floor, but I got some boards and laid them across the opening and made a floor, and then, with a chair for furniture, I used the shaft as a place of prayer.

Whenever the mill was running smoothly, I could go into this sanctuary with my Bible, and close the door. Many hours every day were spent there in prayer and Bible study. The sound of the machinery was all I needed to tell me when something was wrong. The superintendent had often found me there reading or praying but never mentioned it.

One day, about two years after my conversion, a small boy came into the mill trying to sell some newspapers. Through pity for the child I bought a copy, and sat down to glance through it and soon became engrossed. Oblivious to the sound of the machinery I read on and on. Finally sensing that something was wrong, I glanced up and saw the superintendent coming toward me holding a handful of "chat tailings" (a term for refuse rock after the ore had been taken from it). There was unextracted ore in it. I knew I merited a severe reprimand, and never again on that job did I read anything but my Bible. It was in Galen that God gave me much of the teaching which in later years I was to give out to multiplied thousands of people.

I remember well Brother Parham's preaching. Himself a personable, gifted, accomplished, original and forceful thinker and a vivid magnetic personality with superb, versatile platform ability, he always held his audience in the curve of his hand.

People sat spellbound, one moment weeping, the next rocking with laughter, as the words flowed from his lips like water gushing from a fountain. But through it all he was sending home with clean, incisive, powerful strokes, the unadulterated Word of God.

His humility, his meekness and consecration impressed everyone most favorably, and he became a father to us all. He took the Work of God *literally and practiced it as such*, teaching us that each command Jesus *ever gave* should be *literally obeyed at any cost*. Prevailing prayer solved every problem, and it was the foundation of all his work.

A former Methodist minister, he had become a licensed exhorter with that group at seventeen years of age. But shortly before I met him, he had declared himself undenominational. As I remember it, the change had come about in this way.

Investigating the different new religious movements which were flourishing just before the turn of the $20^{th}$ Century, he had some to see more light in the Word of God than ever before.

Dr. Dowie and Dr. Sanford preached Divine Healing, but preached Sanctification as being also the Baptism of the Holy Ghost. Some of their teaching he believed and saw clearly, but to some he had no witness in his heart. Everyone seemed especially confused on the evidence of the Holy Ghost Baptism.

# Chapter 5

While living in Topeka, Kansas, a few years prior to the Pentecostal outpouring, Reverend Parham had gathered a good congregation around the truths of Divine Healing, Sanctification (much as Dr. Simpson had taught it), and the Baptism of the Holy Ghost, but without possessing any definite seal or sign from God, as he was to teach later.

He had established Bethel Healing Home, a sort of combination hotel and Bible School, where the sick were brought to be cared for and healed by the Lord.

While Brother Parham was away on a trip of investigation, searching for new truths, his supply pastor had appropriated for himself the large healing home and the congregation as well. Accepting Scripture literally as he did, he let it all go rather than break the Lord's command, "Resist not evil," Matt 5:39, and thus disrupt the saints.

Following God's leading, Reverend Parham then issued an invitation to all ministers and Christians everywhere (who were willing to forsake all, sell or give away what they owned, and enter a Bible-School for study, prayer, and waiting upon God) to come together in Topeka where they would unitedly trust God daily for all their living expenses. The sole declared purpose of this school was to encourage and fit workers to go everywhere preaching "this Gospel of the Kingdom" (which he was convinced had never been preached in these latter days in its fullness, Matthew 24:14)… "as a witness to all nations" before the end of the age, and to receive God's promised power for such a labor of love.

Reverend Parham was already issuing a paper by faith twice a month, called *The Apostolic Faith*. The paper bore as the subscription price, the Scripture "Isaiah 55:1."

To house this new school, the Lord gave them what was known in Topeka as "The Old Stone Mansion." It was a magnificent structure for those days, and was very grand indeed. It had been patterned after the style of an English castle and was, I believe, built of white stone with a red brick trim. It had beautifully carved doors, woodwork and stairs, and was lavishly finished in different rare and expensive woods, imported cedar of Lebanon, bird's eye maple, spotted pine, cherry, mahogany, and other handsome materials.

Atop this commodious four story residence was an observatory and lookout on the highest point. It was reached by an outside winding stair. Cupolas and turrets decorated the rest of the building-one of these rooms being large enough for what they christened "The Prayer Tower."

There in the Prayer Tower, volunteer students kept a watch of three hours each, so that prayer was constantly being made for the furtherance of God's Kingdom here on earth. Those who wished to spend the entire night in prayer were allowed to do so.

Around forty Christians answered Reverend Parham's call, and the school, known as the "College of Bethel" was opened in October 1900. This assembled fellowship was not the usual young student body attending a Bible college. They were a company of older people-returned missionaries and a few elderly saints-all in all, a company who had been stirred alike by the signs of the times and unknowingly had been chosen by the Lord for this very purpose.

Reverend Parham had been very stirred over the doctrine of the Baptism of the Holy Ghost, but he found few Christians who agreed on any one special evidence. Some held that the "laying on of hands" was the correct way to receive Him; some thought that Sanctification was the seal; some claimed it "by faith"; but none claimed any certain evidence as its major witness.

Reverend Parham was deeply convinced that the Church as a whole should now go before the world with a Scriptural evidence which was indubitably Biblical; that for us there was a power, judging from God's promises which the church in general had not yet received. It was to this search of the Scriptures that the College of Bethel dedicated itself.

By December of 1900 they had reached in their studies the second chapter of Acts and were confronted with the important question: "What, if any, was the true Biblical sign of the Baptism of the Holy Ghost, and how could Christians be certain they had received it?"

For days the subject of evidence was exhaustively discussed in and out of classes. Various opinions were held, yet no one seemed really satisfied that his own opinion was the correct one. Seeing this confusion of ideas, Reverend Parham finally proposed that they let God settle it.

They were told to take their Bibles and go to their separate rooms alone, and to fast and pray and wait upon the Lord, seeking Him for the truth. They were to consider this question before God for three full days undisturbed. At the end of that time they were to meet again and report their findings.

At the end of the allotted period, when they had assembled once more, it was found that, without any exception, God had convinced each one of them separately and unequivocally, during their solitude, as they waited upon His knowledge and wisdom alone, that the only Scriptural evidence which invariably accompanied the Baptism of the Holy Ghost as recorded in the Bible, was speaking in "tongues" as the Spirit gave them utterance.

The entire school had to acknowledge that none of them, despite all their previous claims, and beliefs, had received such a Baptism. So, they decided to seek God to be truly that is, Scripturally-filled with the Holy Ghost.

In the church world just before the turn of the century, ministers in their pulpits, and Christians everywhere, with the press to publicize it, had all been impressed by God through the importance of the approaching new century. Everyone was stirred. Much was made of it. Prophesies, strange to ordinary ears, were being suddenly discussed, although not perfectly understood by the majority of Christians. Some were reported in the daily papers as thinking that the "Epiphany" –whatever that was! –might occur in the approaching 20th Century. Feeling ran high. Yet everyone seemed sure that some strange thing, some phenomenon, would undoubtedly take place as the new century dawned.

Of this particular New Year's Eve at the turn of the century, my wife relates the following.

I remember well this New Year's Eve in our Southern town. My father, who always retired early, would usually, on New Year's Eve, begin to doze off and finally slip into bed, apologetically asking my mother to waken him at midnight.

But not this night! All over our house lights blazed! No one slept! No one even talked! There was a tenseness in the very atmosphere, an expectancy which I, child that I was, could not understand too well. As the dragging, hurrying hours went slowly by, each tick of the clock seemed to set the pace for the beat of my excitedly responding heart. All our neighbors next door, the leader of the women's work in another church, left her own family group and approached us.

"I feel as if the Magi and their camels might suddenly come riding down the street!" she said, half laughingly.

"And I, too," agreed my mother in her more serious manner.

They stood quietly for a while, each sharing the other's emotion. Then my mother spoke in a hushed, almost reverent tone:

"I shouldn't be surprised if the heavens opened at midnight and the angels sang."

"Nor I," replied our neighbor.

A few minutes longer they stood together watching the darkness and the sky, as the minutes went by. Then slowly they drifted back to their tensely waiting families. Solemnly we all sat on until midnight. But nothing happened: no angels, no magi, nothing but extra guns, extra bells, and extra whistles.

My father, who was not a follower of the Lord, announced flatly immediately after midnight, with a quizzical look in his eye:

"Well, *I'm* going to bed!"

Was he, too, disappointed? I thought so, but I could not be sure. My mother finally sighed, relaxed and said in a low impressive tone:

"We shall hear of this. God had done something somewhere, and we shall surely hear of it!"

# Chapter 6

It was New Year's Eve.

A clock ticked rhythmically-steadily.

Swiftly the minutes which were bearing a world relentlessly onward to the close of its Nineteenth Century flew by. It was a momentous evening! 9:30! 10:00! 10:30! Silently… swiftly… unavoidably the last few hours of the century moved magnetically onward to its grand completion. It was an evening full of portent!

With a feeling of awe tinged with fear, people everywhere were alertly watching the passing of this particular year, as it fled on swift feet into a boundless infinity.

Many a troubled mind strove anxiously to pierce the intervening veil which the future held pinned so securely, but beheld instead only baffling mystery shrouded in darkness. Speculation was rife.

What might one expect of a brand new century? What changes might it not bring? Would there be a new order of things upon the earth? Who knew but that the end of the world might even come! These were some of the questions discussed.

This was a momentous evening for the entire Christian world! Weary children who had for once been allowed to sit up and wait for the boom of the big guns, the crack of the anvils, and the ringing of delirious bells, nodded sleepy heads and drooped weary eyelids grown heavy with waiting.

The wide stretching Kansas plains lay dreaming under the cold, crisp light of the white stars, and in the streets of the little city of Topeka, lights twinkled…

Within their homes family groups sat here and there, amusing themselves quietly, families who were accustomed to far much earlier retirement from the cares of the day.

10:30! 11:00! 11:30! For many it was a solemn evening, full of foreboding.

In other places merriment ran high. Tinkling music and dancing feet set the pace, while the youth of the little city swept carelessly on through the night in lighthearted gaiety...some even in unrestrained, unchristian revelry and laxity.

But in one of the large rooms of the great house known as "The Old Stone Mansion," formerly the official residence of governors long gone, I am told, a different scene was being enacted.

Blazing chandeliers lit up a scene of worship... of adoration...of devotion! People knelt, or sat quietly about the room, naturally, unaffectedly, as people do who have devoted themselves wholly to one purpose.

And that was exactly what they had done! For three weeks they had been waiting there...praying...Believing...scarcely knowing what to expect...and yet following undauntedly the torch of faith, which had been planted within their bosoms.

Three weeks! Three glorious weeks in which Heaven seemed to stoop down and touch the earth...in which the Son of God had walked among them and opened to them the Scriptures! "He shall baptize *you* with the Holy Ghost and fire!"

How was one to know? Was there to be no sign? Could so important a manifestation of the presence of God take place without one's scarcely knowing it? Without even one of the signs which had originally accompanied it? They prayed on!

11:30…11:45…midnight!

Soon over the assembled company there came the passing of the Divine Breath! A woman began to quiver slightly…the rhythmic quivering of a leaf rippled by the wind…and beautifully, forcefully, distinctly there tripped from her lips ecstatic utterances which soon became a language…unintelligible to the kneeling company…but without doubt a language! Acts 2 and 4! Could it be possible!

Rising to investigate the phenomenon further, they beheld a blue flame like fire playing about her head, as she gladly and joyfully yielded herself completely to the Holy Spirit of God.

>  "O spread the tidings round!
> Wherever man is found!
> Wherever human hearts
> And human woes abound;
> Let every Christian tongue
> Proclaim the joyful sound-
> The Comforter has come!
> The Comforter has come!
> The Comforter has come!
> The Holy Ghost from Heaven,
> The Father's promise given;
> O spread the tidings round
> Wherever man is found!
> The Comforter has come!"

Truly God had done something! Although the many little groups of watchers scattered over the country saw it not, God had ordained that as the next few decades slowly passed, the whole world would hear of what He had done on that New Year's Day at the turn of that century.

"And it shall come to pass that at evening time it shall be light." Zach. 14:7.

# Chapter 7

In the College of Bethel at Topeka, momentous events were indeed taking place and God's Spirit was hovering over them in preparation for a divine manifestation of His Presence.

The rest of this little group of called-out-ones now decided that they themselves must first have the true Baptism of the Holy Ghost before they could attempt to carry such good news to others, reasoning that if their conclusion were correct, God would undoubtedly confirm their own baptism with Bible signs following.

So for days they had waited before Him, fasting, praying, praising, and acknowledging His Sovereignty, and the Sovereignty of His Word.

On that night a congregation of about seventy-five saints met with the school for the evening service. God seemed very close. During a prolonged prayer, Miss Agnes N. Ozman, a returned missionary, requested them to lay hands upon her as an act of dedication and pray for her that she might receive the Pentecostal fullness promised to all "believers."

They had prayed but a few sentences of the prayer of dedication, when she quietly began speaking in Chinese, nor could she speak anything else for three days. She could not even write English...only Chinese. Copies of this writing were published in various daily newspapers and her experience attracted considerable attention. Those who watched all said that when the glory of God fell, it played like a halo of light about her face and head.

For three more days the college sat in His presence and waited upon God. They prayed through to where they knew that He was coming in power, and then they waited for him, "lost in wonder, love and praise," occasionally singing and making melody in worship unto the Lord.

Then on the night of January 3, simultaneously, during a public service, twelve ordained ministers of various faiths also received the Holy Ghost and spoke in tongues, while a Heavenly brightness, above any natural light, filled the room.

Some of those who were seeking were sitting, some were kneeling, and some were standing with upraised hands, but there was no violent emotion, although some trembled slightly. Tongues of fire sat upon their heads. Finally, in unison, the ministers all began to sing "Jesus, Lover of my soul" in at least six different languages, but with what sounded to the listeners like angelic voices.

When all this "was noised abroad," the crowds began to gather. Newspaper reporters from cities as far away as St. Louis, Missouri, came to see and hear. They were convinced and wrote front page reports with large headlines for the big dailies. Soon other reporters brought along government interpreters, professors of languages, and even foreigners, to hear and identify the languages being spoken through human beings by the Spirit of God.

The modest, Christian behavior of these students, coupled with the undeniable fact that they were all speaking known languages with correct accent and intonation, caused all who saw and heard to praise them at that time.

And so, day after day, student after student was caught up into the glory and scripturally sealed with the Holy Ghost, "speaking with other tongues," exactly as the apostles had done on the Day of Pentecost.

# Chapter 8

The Lord had been talking to my heart about His work for some time, but I felt I could never be qualified for such an honor, so from time to time I put Him off with excuses.

One Sunday morning after having dressed for Sunday School, I hurriedly went out to water my horse. Father had a horse in the same stable, and on this day there was a slack rope which formed a partition between the two horses. Carrying a pail of water, I stepped over the rope and, in my haste, awkwardly caught my toe and fell to the ground. The pail of water slipped from my hand and rolled against the horse's heels. Kicking at the pail, she struck my face. She had been newly shod the day before and one of the new corks caught in my eye, while the toe of the shoe struck my jaw, tearing it open. As the blow came, I knew instantly why it had happened. Just as I lost sensibility a Voice said: "This is your last chance."

"Yes, Lord, I'll go," I answered.

When I regained consciousness, I got up and went into the house. Mother was shocked when she saw my face torn and covered with blood. She and the Church prayed for me. On Thursday, when I went to the barbershop to get a shave, the barber looked at me and said: "I heard that you had been seriously injured last Sunday. It must have been a mistake." I showed him the scar and told him how God had a mistake.

When I had finished high school, I went back to the mines and took charge of a large plant about six miles from Galena, driving a horse and rig back and forth every night and morning. My mother began attending the meetings with me; soon she also was converted.

Then we attended the services together and how supremely happy we were in the Lord!

As a result of the Galen revival, an Assembly was established on Third Street called the Third Street Mission, which we attended for about two years.

By that time Joplin, Missouri and Columbus, Melrose, Galena and Baxter Springs in Kansas all had established churches to which we went often, for we attended a service nearly every night.

In the summer of 1905, Reverend Parham took a band of twenty-four workers to Houston, Texas to open a work. Soon a great revival was on. Mrs. Mary Arthur and Mrs. Fannie Dobson were left in charge of the Galena Assembly.

Then in September of 1905, a Camp Meeting was held in Columbus, Kansas. I took two weeks off from my job and attended. The Pentecostal work was now spreading throughout this section of the country and large groups gathered for the Camp. Wonderful things happened there also. Some of the workers who had gone South were back, and all were in attendance, victorious, happy and filled with the Spirit. They told how the Lord had worked in the field. This overjoyed all our hearts.

A second group was now preparing to go to Texas to assist in opening more works. At the close of the Columbus Camp, a company of twenty-two workers was ready to go to Texas for active evangelistic training.

True to my promise, I sold my horse, rig and everything I had, and bought a ticket to Houston. I gave the remaining funds to the general treasury, since we were to have all things in common.

Thus, I started out with my pockets empty of money, but my heart brimful of zeal and courage for the Lord. It was really a step of faith for all of us, dependent upon God alone as we were. But we felt that if He had led us to go, He would care for us, and thanks be to Him, He has never failed through all these years.

On the way down to Houston we changed trains at Alvin, Texas, and laid over for a few hours. During the noon hour we went uptown and held a street meeting. A large, hospitable crowd quickly gathered, manifesting great interest in the "new religion." Hungrily, they pressed us to come back again.

To welcome the arrival of this second band in Houston, Special Convocation of workers had been arranged for a short time only. During their stay in Houston we heard many of the remarkable things the Lord had been doing in the Texas field.

They had just come from a revival in Orchard, Texas, where a big ranch owner, a Brother Ayler, was sympathetic with our message and had backed the work in Orchard. He had previously contacted Reverend Parham about coming to Texas, and the first meeting had been held there. He later became fully Pentecostal and supported the cause with his influence and finances. Their second meeting took place in Houston.

The outstanding feature of the revival held in Huston's "Bryan Hall" was the remarkable healings. One was a lawyer's wife, a Mrs. Denlaney, who had been seriously injured in a street car accident and who, as a consequence, had considerable publicity in the law courts of Houston, due to her resultant paralysis. When she was miraculously healed, she and her cure attracted the attention of the entire city.

At the end of the Houston Convocation all of us were separated and put into companies of five to eight workers with a man and his wife acting as chaperons for each company.

I was sent back to Alvin with a former Baptist minister, Brother Oscar Jones, of Kansas, as leader of our band. He rented the Opera House and we began our campaign. In a few days the Lord Jesus began to manifest Himself and the town's people received us gladly.

Soon we needed a larger hall. We rented what had once been a storage building. We moved into this as the revival kept increasing in power and interest...and results.

There were many young people here who were filled with the Holy Ghost and had spoken in other tongues "for a sign." Many of these also received a call to the Lord's work. Among them were Walter Jessup, Hugh Cadwalder and his sister, Rosa, Hattie Allen, Millicent McClendon, and others.

The power of God was so great in the alter services here that the seekers often fell as if they were dead, and would lie immovable for hours, only their lips whispering softly to God. Early in the mourning they would have to be piled like cord-wood into the back of a delivery wagon and taken home to continue their solitary soul's search after God. These usually came through to a glowing experience right in their own homes. A thriving Pentecostal church was the result of this revival. Alvin had now become another established revival center for us, for which we thanked God.

A second Company of workers had been sent on to the seaside resort of Galveston, which was a few miles beyond Alvin. They were having a hard, spiritual battle in Galveston, so fresh workers were sent down to assist them from Houston, which was fifty miles inland. I was sent to them from Alvin. Brother and Sister George Rose, Sarah Bradbury, Cora Lane and others were among the group in Galveston. Their leader was Tommy Miller.

Galveston was a very wicked place at that time; it was full of spiritualists and many other spirits of evil. We soon realized that we were battling against great spiritual darkness, and our faith was severely tested in many ways. As we were often without money or food, most of our time was spent in fasting and in prayer.

It was an inflexible rule of ours that no public offerings of any kind could be taken in at any of our meetings; neither were we allowed to mention our needs. We mentioned only our general system of financing our work, whether privately or publicly. Thus we had to trust God alone for all our needs, accepting only tithes and gifts given to us as unto God. With this system of financing, we felt that God could more easily permit us to be tested for our own development whenever we needed it.

But later, after we had established a fully functioning church, the church itself decided its own method of financing, but as far as I know, none ever gave their pastor a salary. These all preferred still to live by faith.

During one of these testing times, while still in Galveston, a friend in Alvin, Brother Carlyle, who was the manager of a produce company which shipped green vegetables to northern markets in the winter, sent us a crate of fresh white table turnips.

Although a residence had been rented for the workers as well as a store building in which to hold meetings, we had no personal money; consequently, we had no fuel with which to cook the turnips. But it was considered shameful to utter a word of complaint for what God chose for us, for we knew that what He did was always best. So we gladly submitted to His will without murmuring.

When mealtime came we would kneel around the dining table and have a period of prayer and worship, in which we returned thanks to the Lord for His love and care for us. There on each plate would be a whole raw turnip which we all ate with grateful hearts. For eight days raw turnips made up our entire menu. The love, the joy and fire with which our hearts were flooded make up for such slight things as lack of food or warmth.

From that day to this I appreciate a turnip, as it never fails to remind me of this time of great spiritual blessing. I have since found, from a standpoint of health, that a raw turnip diet is excellent.

It was at Galveston that I learned another lesson. I thought perhaps that I should do what I naturally could to relieve our needy situation. So, Brother Miller and I borrowed an expensive deep-sea fishing throw-line, waded out through the shallow water into the Gulf of Mexico until we came to some great rocks, and prepared to cast from there.

I had been told to tie the fishing line to my body as it might slip away from me, but I neglected to do this. I cast a few times and then once again. This time I flung my line with all my strength far out into the ocean. The end of the line which I had carelessly wrapped around my fingers slipped off and the entire tackle sailed out into the sea, past hope of recovery.

Disappointed, disgusted with myself, hungry, and sick at heart over the loss of the borrowed line, I decided from then on to "let patience have her perfect work," and not try to help the Lord.

I then began to realize more fully than ever that God was purposely sending whatever might happen to us, and that it was allowed only for the good of his children.

So far, I have said little of our prayer life. When food was withheld, God seemed closest. Truly the Holy Ghost "helped our infirmities." There was constant prayer! Earnest… fervent…deep…pungent…searching…full………..... of faith…full……….of…….love……...and compassion…importunate…prevailing prayer! Prayer that moved both Heaven and earth! There was prayer the like of which we had never seen before! "Then did my heart rejoice, and my lips sing His wondrous praise!" because I had lived to see this glorious Day of the Lord.

# Chapter 9

Later, in the fall of 1905, the workers were called off the field to attend a short-term Bible and Training School which convened in "Caledonia Hall" on Texas Avenue near Main Street in Houston.

As usual, we were given a thorough workout and a rigid training in prayer, fasting consecration, Bible study and evangelistic work. Our week day schedule consisted of Bible Study in the morning, shop and jail meetings at noon, house to house visitations in the afternoon, and six o'clock street meeting followed by an evening evangelistic service at 7:30 or 8:00 o'clock.

The Southern Pacific Railroad shops offered a great opportunity to preach to large crowds of men at noon. Many of these men found salvation, Brother Joe Roselli among them.

By this time there was a good-sized congregation of saints in the Houston church.

The Reverend, W. Fay Carrothers, a former Methodist minister, then pastor of an Independent Holiness Church in Brunner, a suburb of Houston, had received his Pentecostal baptism the year before this school took place. He was now the Pastor of the Houston Assembly, and under God, became a great blessing to this school by his godly example and excellent teaching.

Our residence and school building was at 503 Rusk Avenue; it was quite a good location in those days. It was near the largest and most beautifully appointed hotel in Houston, which is still called the "Rice Hotel."

Among ourselves, we students laughingly dubbed our residence the "Rice Hotel," because almost all we could afford to eat that entire winter was rice.

However, the Lord was in that school in a mighty way, so much so that He seemed to be leading it Himself. The lack of food and the constant rice diet did not seem to bother anyone.

In order to attract the attention of the crowds to the Gospel, Reverend Parham would often have the workers dress, sometimes even for street meetings, in Palestinian costumes, flowing robes, dazzling colors and all. He explained as he spoke what country or district the robe speakers represented.

He had previously bought some of these costumes to use in lecture work and they were very effective in attracting crowds. Our leader was a most versatile and entertaining speaker, and while explaining the garments, he could get in enough Gospel to impress any man. It was rare indeed for anyone ever to leave while he was speaking.

One night, in a watch night service back in Galena, I had heard him preach to a large audience for five hours without stopping, and no one apparently had moved or left the service until he had finished.

About this time a colored woman named Lucy Farrow, who was engaged as a cook at the School, was feeling a burden for Los Angeles. After receiving the Spirit's Baptism during this School in Houston, she felt the call of God upon her. Brother Parham provided the money for her fare from our treasury, and she left for the West Coast.

She started a prayer meeting in Los Angeles, so we were told, and the Lord began to pour out His Spirit. Soon she wrote back to Houston and asked that someone be sent to assist her.

A colored Baptist preacher from Houston was selected – a Brother Seymour, who had often attended the morning sessions of the School, and had received the light of the Pentecostal message in it's fullness, but had not as of yet been filled with the Spirit.

In answer to Sister Farrow's call for help, money was again raised by the School in order to send Brother Seymour to Los Angeles. When he arrived there he found that God was working mightily, for the Los Angeles outpouring of April 1906 was already under way. He became a prominent leader for a while in the old Azusa Street work.

When news of this great outpouring was noised abroad, hundreds of ministers, Christian workers and missionaries came from all parts of the continent to Los Angeles to see what it was all about. Many of them humbled themselves before God, sought His face and were filled with the Holy Spirit, speaking in tongues as in Acts 2:4. Many of them later became widely known leaders in our work, such as: A. H. Argue, "R. E." McAllister, A.G. Garr, Glen Cook, E. J. Ewart, Frank Small, A. G. Canada, Frank Bartleman, Max Morehead, Harry Morse, John Sinclair, and William H. Durham were among them. Mrs. Crawford and Mrs. Lum were also some of the workers who visited Los Angeles at that time and witnessed God's power in the Azusa Street meetings. The last two workers mentioned soon founded the Apostolic Faith Mission on Burnside Street in Portland, OR.

Not long after, some of the believers in charge of the Azusa work, allowed various kings of fleshly manifestations to creep in under the impression that they were of God. But these later proved to be unwholesome and thus hindered their work. Fanaticism then made it's appearance, and for a while was allowed to run unchecked.

Brother Parham heard of these extremes and later made a trip to Los Angeles, hoping to help the workers to steady the work. But, as is often the case, they felt that they had received a greater power in Los Angeles than had been known before, so Brother Parham's saving advice and counsel went unheeded and rejected.

However, many good healthy Assemblies were springing up all over the continent which were led by men of discernment, and the Pentecostal truth was spreading all over the world. God had undertaken to establish His Truth, and nothing could stop it.

The Houston School closed in the Spring of 1906 and we all went to our different fields of labor filled with God's Spirit, more determined than ever to scatter this Latter Rain message of salvation far and near.

It was our custom as we went to the night meetings to march down the center of the main street two abreast, singing evangelistic hymns. There was no motor traffic in those days and the horses by that time of evening were safely in their stables for the night. Thus the street was open, while the sidewalks were generally congested. This marching therefore attracted much attention to our work and paid off in advertising.

Usually a large banner proclaiming "Apostolic Faith Movement" was carried aloft by two young men at the head of the marching column. With a band of fifty to seventy young people on fire for the Lord and a capable and colorful leader, the city soon knew we were there.

We received excellent training. For lessons in poise, we were put out by ourselves to conduct a street meeting, each one of us having been instructed previously in our own part.

As the meeting progressed, our leader would sometimes unexpectedly appear in the back of the crowd, which had gathered and, as stranger would in those days, begin to heckle us unmercifully. Sometimes he would be disputing the Scriptures we were preaching – sometimes privately to those around him, or making fun of us, but always trying to publicly confuse and disconcert the worker speaking. Soon we all were able to go on with our service, no matter what happened, no matter what the distraction, no matter what stumbling block might be put in our way.

On the other hand, when we were unable by our hand efforts to attract a crowd, our leader would take his place among us and begin preaching. From the time he uttered his first few words, the crowd would begin to gather from all directions until the street would be packed. As soon as he had a crowd for us, he would usually disappear, and allow the students to finish the service.

We did not wear uniforms. The lady workers dressed in the current fashions of the day…silks…satins…jewels or whatever they happened to possess. They were very smartly turned out, so that they made a very impressive appearance on the streets where a large part of our work was conducted in the early years.

It was not until long after, when former Holiness preachers had become a part of us, that strict plainness of dress began to be taught.

Although Entire Sanctification was preached at the beginning of the Movement, it was from a Wesleyan viewpoint and had in it very little of the later Holiness Movement characteristics. Nothing was ever said about apparel, for everyone was so taken up with the

Lord that mode of dress seemingly never occurred to any one of us.

It would be difficult indeed, to describe adequately the spiritual aspect of these Schools for you, but it seems necessary to attempt it.

When we first gathered we began by seeking the face of the Lord almost day and night. Of course, that was our usual way of life – everyone lived in His presence constantly. But when we gathered for a School, we sought Him for special guidance, blessing, teaching, and power for that particular time and locality, and for all whom we might touch or influence.

In reply to a few days or hours of earnest, conscientious seeking, and unselfish surrender to His will, God's spirit always settled down upon us.

We were peculiarly fused together by the Spirit as a whole, so that at times it seemed that we were dealt with almost as one person. A deep hush lay upon our souls… a kind of breathless suspension when everything earthly disappeared and we were lifted up to a Heavenly locale and brought to attention before God in the Spirit, in a restful, holy, quiet intentness upon His every word and mood.

This seemed to me to be most like resting upon a cloud before God, basking in the very nearness of the Savior and in the sunshine of His smile.

The feeling of His immediate presence was everywhere. Particularly did He fill the assembly room or church where we met for worship. The School usually ran from 9 a.m. to around 4 p.m. or whenever the Spirit released us. Usually our dinner was served around 5 o' clock and by 6:30 p.m. we were on the streets, ready to start service. A kind of glorious awe filled us always; it made us speak often in hushed voices, and go softly and sweetly even about our daily task.

At times He thrilled us as by an electrical surcharging, but most often it was simply the luxury of His exquisite love, a deep thrilling along every nerve of spirit, soul, and body, experiences rich in emotion, in promise, and in fulfillment.

At such seasons of worship, things of the world and of time faded from our vision, and we might as easily have been sitting with Moses on a stone upon Mount Sinai's summit, so completely were we closed in with God.

Then one was often conscious of the pressure of the Spirit filling the atmosphere above, of either dipping and gently caressing us, or of lifting us up, one or several at a time, into a glory that was pure intoxication. Yet at other times during the evening or Sunday services, volumes of praise to God would arise spontaneously from hundreds of throats as full and resonant as the sound of many waters tossed in a resounding sea. And the singing! It was not we alone who sang them Again it was the "Spirit that helped our infirmities," and angelic host that sang with us.

Hundreds of people, over the years, have mentioned that it was not earthly but heavenly music.

There were hours of teaching through heavily anointed ministers, or through tongues and interpretation and, more rarely, through straight prophecy.

Difficult passages of Scripture might be given; there were personal reproofs, but seldom was there praise. Perhaps there were instructions concerning the handling of God's work in the field, of about daily living and holiness. But, above all, there was the assurance needs and perplexities. He was dear, loved Father to us and we were His obedient children-raven-fed and supplied. We saw Jesus only.

# Chapter 10

Near the close of this Houston Camp Meeting of School, a group of workers was sent to Wallis, Texas, to open a work. Tommy Miller, Walter Jessup, Nora Byrd, Mabel Wise, Millicent McClendon and Hattie Allen comprised the group sent there. I was with them part of the time, but I soon returned to Houston.

A young German Brother and I were sent out, instructed only to go South toward the Gulf of Mexico and stop anywhere we could find a place to preach. For capital to launch our project, our leader gave us a silver dollar apiece-all that he had left. At last we were on our own as evangelists. We went to Alvin and received a little money, and thus reinforced, arrived in Angleton, Texas, on February 27, 1906.

A room in the Angleton Hotel cost us fifty cents a day. The Court House Auditorium was free for a few meetings, and there we opened the first Gospel meeting of which I had ever had full charge.

We soon found an old abandoned saloon building which we could use regularly. As we had received no more money, we borrowed planks of new lumber from the lumber yard for seat, and laid them across a few of the empty, up-ended kegs which had been left in the building. When the building was cleaned and ready for us, we set out to get a crowd, but we had little success at first.

This meeting was a long, hard pull for it did not break as quickly as the others had. Much of the time we were without food-once for three days, as I recall. But that did not deter us, for we were so blessed spiritually, and so happy to be working for the Lord that we scarcely noticed it.

Each night there were about thirteen people in the congregation, each one seated on one end of the thirteen plank seats, so that they could support a shoulder against the wall. Others stood outside and looked in, but only these thirteen would enter. I preached every night for seven weeks before a break came, but when God did begin to do things, the bottom of Heaven seemed to fall out. Of course, after that we were soon abundantly supplied with food and lodgings.

Addison Mercer, a deacon in the Baptist Church who thought he had salvation but found that he hadn't, was our first convert. The day after his conversion he took several big chickens back to a neighbor saying he had stolen them.

Since he had been considered one of the best Christians in town, the community was really shocked when the news got around. But such spectacular conversion as his and others surely did have their effect.

They were all deeply sincere; they covered up nothing, and held back nothing. This brought everyone under conviction and packed the building. Brother Mercer later became an Apostolic Faith preacher himself.

The Angleton revival spread to mighty proportions. Scores were saved, healed and filled with the Spirit. We obtained a tent for summer work, and the country for miles around was stirred to seek God. Many signs and wonders were also done in Angleton by the Spirit of the Lord.

While this meeting was in progress a Convention was announced to convene at Ochard, Texas, for April

13-15 Easter weekend. All the preachers and workers who could plan to attend. I went from Angleton with the purpose in my heart to seek the Lord with prayer and fasting until He filled me with the Holy Ghost. I had a wonderful anointing's in teaching and preaching the word of God. At other times I had been so blessed that it seemed that I had everything but the speaking in other tongues; but I knew by the Word of God that, when I would be fully baptized in the Holy Spirit, I would speak in other languages.

I sought the Lord constantly both day and night throughout the entire Convention. At 2:00 o'clock, Monday morning, April 16th, I was still not filled with the overflowing measure. Disappointed, I walked, late though it was, beyond the edge of the little town, and kneeling down under a small mesquite tree, prayed until 7:00 a.m. that morning, when the train was due which would take us back to our various appointments.

This train was more than an hour overdue and about 100 of us were at the depot waiting. Brother Parham suggested that we have some singing. Then, after some of the crowd had testified, Brother Parham began to preach. He was still preaching when the train rolled in, carrying two extra coaches for our workers. We were so blessed by God that the only thing we wanted to do was to rejoice, pray, and praise the Lord.

The coach which I boarded was filled with our group, all praying and worshipping God, and soon the Lord really began to pour out His Spirit upon us. That coach became a veritable prayer room! Some were kneeling at their seats, some had their hands uplifted in worship, and some were standing. Still others were praying with seekers, for God was now baptizing them with His precious Holy Spirit, and they were talking in tongues as the Spirit spoke through them.

I knew that several had already been filled when suddenly the power of God struck me! I was so grateful. Soon the power and fire of God came heavier and heavier upon me, until it seemed to me that I must really be on fire! This fire and power, coming upon me for the first time in my life, seemed to melt all my natural strength, leaving me lying helplessly back in my seat. With every compartment of my mind fully surrendered to God, I told the Lord to have His way with me, as I was completely relaxed, He did. Oh, such joy and glory! I had never dreamed it could be! Soon my English stopped and I could talk and praise no more.

As I lay back limply against my chair, the Spirit of God took possession of my fully surrendered body, and lastly took hold of my throat and vocal chords in what to me was a new and strange way. God's power and glory upon me became far greater than I have ever since been able to describe.

This went on for several minutes, while the fire of God flamed hotter and hotter, until I thought that I must be actually on fire. When another great volt of God's lightning struck me, thereby loosening me still further, I began to speak in strange tongues as the Spirit actually did the speaking. I talked first in one language, which was soon changed to another, and then to another. I could tell when the change in the language came because they were so different. I sat there completely relaxed, even helpless, and let the Lord control me Himself, as the different languages came and went.

About the same time that I had begun to speak, I heard a young lady from Angleton – Miss Marry Smith, who with her mother, was seated facing me – also begin to speak on another tongue. They both had been waiting for the Holy Ghost in Angleton as well as I. What a time we all had in the Lord! What a train ride!

Too soon the time came when some of us had to change trains in order to catch the southbound train for Angleton. In our coach I later found that the Lord had immersed twelve of us, as the Greek text defines "Baptism," truly saturating, dipping, plunging us into the Holy Ghost. Five in the next coach had gone through a similar experience. Many had to leave the train at this particular junction, to change from the main Sante Fe line to another railroad which crossed at this point.

I was so filled with the Spirit that when I stood up, I could scarcely keep my feet on the ground. Neither had I the power to speak in English. Since our train was late, we had missed our planned connection, and I needed to give instructions to our group as to what course we would follow in this emergency. I knew the train we wanted to board was down at a sugar plantation about a mile and a half away, since it took on freight there before going farther south. It would be possible, if there happened to be enough freight, to catch the train there. An old man with a team of a light express wagon stood near. After trying to speak English, I finally had to make signs to him to get the women and the baggage down to the plantation junction immediately.

After he had loaded, he whipped up the mules and started them at a run, while I ran down the track ahead of them to try and hold the train. As I went down that railroad track I was so exhilarated that it seemed as though I were flying; that the Spirit of the Lord had come upon me just as it had upon Elijah when he ran before Ahab's chariot. It seemed as if I were taking about twenty feet with each step. Perhaps I actually did; I'll never know.

As it was level country the train crew could see us coming so they held the train until we all got aboard. The Lord filled five more of our company with His Spirit on that train also. When we arrived in Angleton, the town soon knew we were there, for we all got off the train Scripturally "drunk" with the Spirit and the power of God.

That night almost the entire community converged on the tent to hear and see what had happened. I had charge of the service but I still could not speak English. I led the song service, but could only sing in another language.

Indeed "our mouths were filled with laughter and our tongues with singing Hosannas!"

When the Lord turned again the captivity of Zion, we were like them that dream! "Then was our mouth filled with laughter, and our tongue with singing; then said they among the heathen, the Lord hath done great things for them!

"The Lord hath done great things for us; whereof we are glad!"

I tried to preach but could not read my Scripture in English. After a few minutes of trying to talk, I finally gave up and motioned the people to the altar. The crowd rushed forward. What praying and power we had! God really walked back and forth through that tent that night! A tremendous volume of praise and prayer went up to God. He poured out His spirit upon many people. I have never seen such a meeting before or since that time.

Night and day the crowds continued to come and what a mighty revival God gave us! Still I could not talk except in other tongues. When I had to go shopping in a store (we didn't starve all the time!), I could only point to what I wanted, and talk in strange tongue because I had no English. God still controlled my tongue.

After more than seven days English gradually returned to me. I think it was almost two weeks before I could preach in English although I tried very hard for the people's sake. For myself, I didn't care. Since I had sought God for nearly two and a half years for this experience, and since the glory and joy were so overpoweringly wonderful, it did not matter to me whether I ever spoke in English again, unless to speak English were in the will of God for me.

When the other languages left, I could speak only in English. Even when I prayed I did not speak in tongues. The power of the Spirit remained in my heart and upon my body, but the tongues had lifted entirely. I regretted this in some measure, but as far as I knew I had done nothing that would displease the Lord. Just why this all should have happened I did not know. It possibly had something to do with my great strength and endurance, which all my life before had been set against God. I could not "yield" myself. God had to teach me how.

The revival did not abate but went on and on, reaping a great harvest of souls.

There were many unusual manifestations of the Spirit at Angleton. Often those who were under the power of God would call for a tablet and write page after page in other languages. Others who had never played a piano in all their lives would go to the instrument and play under the power of the Spirit as skillfully and perfectly as though they had been highly trained; nor could they play again after the anointing had lifted. A great many miracles and notable healings took place as well, more than in some other revivals, largely because the contact with God was so real.

I learned here that prayers and praise is the spiritual road to the presence of God; that the throne of God is hidden in the secret Kingdom of God, kept safely from enemy interference or intrusion, so that only the hungry, conscientious, humble spirit can find the "door" that leads into the secluded realm of the Spirit.

When, with closed eyes and bended knees, the world is left behind, while one's whole being is given over to searching for the passageway from time into the Eternity where our Savior now dwells, angelic help is given to move one along the avenue of prayer to the actual throne-into the presence of the Christ.

Once there, the Lord Jesus quickly lifts the little sin-bruised, child-hearted suppliant into His arms, and lays its head on His bosom. The weary soul is now comforted, and at peace. No matter how world-weary one may have become, this miracle will still occur.

Visiting ministers soon came to assist us to reap this harvest, and they were a great blessing to the newly-formed church. Fay Corrothers, Mable Smith-Hall, Mrs. Annie Hall and several other early workers were among them.

# Chapter 11

Through the years we all learned much more about the Biblical manifestation of "unknown" tongues than we knew then.

Statistics hold that there are over 5,000 different languages and dialects spoken on the earth. Paul says that there are also "tongues of men and of angels." Perhaps there is only one language common to angels, perhaps many. It seems that the latter is true because of the plural form of the word "tongues." Be that as it may, there are enough different languages spoken on this planet alone that, if God so willed, the Holy Ghost could furnish each Christian with a distinct and recognizable language, although it were unknown to the individual receiving it.

Languages spoken by the Holy Ghost through Spirit-filled people have been understood so many times that it is no longer of any not amongst us. We have had ample proof over an extended period of time that the trouble with "doubting Thomases" however, is not with the ability, nor with the accomplishments of God's Spirit, but with our own predilections, our own preconceived ideas.

Mainly I have spoken only in one language through the Spirit, but in that language I was understood by the Armenians in Austin, Texas, who said I spoke fluently in their native tongue.

A Baptist minister, a friend of mine, understood the superintendent of one of our Sunday Schools who spoke in purest Greek, while testifying in one of our services. It was explained to the minister that this man was speaking solely by the unction and inspiration of the Holy Ghost.

It could be said of some: "Among the chief rulers many believed in Him, but because of the Pharisees they did not confess Him, lest they should be put out of the Synagogue; for they loved the praise of men, more than the praise of God."

What a loss! What an irreparable loss has been theirs, when all these years they might have been watching God gloriously at work in His hospital, in His repair shop, in His spiritual filling station, as I was privileged to do. But they will never realize what they have missed until Eternity dawns.

Once when Brother E. N. Bell was preaching in southeastern Missouri, he preached awhile in tongues, "as the Sprit gave utterance." After the service some Russian coal miners from the Ural Mountains who were working in nearby coal mines waited for him outside the tent and tried to talk with him in their native tongue in which he had been speaking. They could scarcely speak English, so were pitiably disappointed when he could not converse with them in their own Russian dialect. Brother Bell tried to explain in English but with little success. It seemed they weren't interested in God's message to them, but only in visiting with someone who could speak their mother tongue.

Although he was a gifted linguist, I never heard Brother Bell speak but that one language by the Spirit. It was so easy to memorize that until this day I remember some of the words and sentences.

One or two of the more presumptuous of the sinner lads, who stood outside during a church service, after hearing brother Bell, would sometimes go down the street speaking parts of Brother Bell's Russian language among themselves. This was sign to them that it was no language at all, for they imagined that any real language would be more difficult for them to master than their own high school Latin.

Many missionaries have had the experience of hearing their adopted tongue spoken by a baptized person while on furlough in this country. But sometimes the opposite occurs.

Pandita Ramabi, of the great school in Lucknow, India, years ago, where as many as two thousand outcast child widows were cared for entirely by faith, records that when receiving the Holy Ghost Baptism many of the believers spoke messages in distinct English, for the most part praising and glorifying God and saying, "He is coming soon."

In his book called "Vision beyond the Veil" H. A. Baker, missionary to China, tells how many little raw heathen orphan boys in his school, when under the anointing of the Spirit, spoke in perfect English, a language with which they were entirely unacquainted. Some of them scripturally described Heaven in English, although they had never heard nor read an account of it at any time, neither had they been indoctrinated. They had been told only to surrender completely to God.

My daughter while praying in tongues in Visual, California, the power of God was falling like rain in blessing upon the congregation. My wife spoke briefly in tongues during a public prayer. A woman near her, also anointed of the Spirit, answered her in tongues. For several minutes they carried on a conversation, their eyes closed, lost in the Spirit. Rising from prayer, Ruth Bernstien-Redmond, the daughter of missionary parents, who herself was born and reared in China, told us that they had both been discussing in perfect Chinese "how wonderful Jesus is."

My wife has been understood many times in Chinese, although she is not confined to that language alone. Since she received the Baptism, she has, over the years, spoken as he moved, in many, many different tongues.

Once while sitting beside a window late in the evening, she heard two men pass on the sidewalk below, conversing in a language which she immediately recognized as one which she most frequently speaks by the Spirit. But she sensed that these were not Pentecostal men speaking by the Spirit of God. I had passed the same men in the street and knew them to be American Indians speaking their own language.

The "gift" of tongues, however, is rare among us. I have been told that years ago, Mrs. Carrie Judd-Montgomery of California, the editor of "Triumphs of Faith," in doing personal work, often stopped foreigners on the street and, at the Spirit's bidding, would begin speaking in their native tongue to them. Although she herself might not know from what country they hailed, she never failed to speak to them in their native dialect. She usually carried on a conversation, and often answered their questions as well. She did this without knowing herself what she was saying. She was much used of God in this way as well as in many others.

In his book with Signs Following, Stanley H. Frodsham relates the story of many fully authenticated miracles, signs, wonders and gifts which took place up to 1926. Many were instances of foreign tongues spoken by the Holy Ghost, many of the "gift" of tongues. One, a Marathi-speaking school teacher of the Mukti Kedgaon Association, "when seeking the Baptism, was given the Guzerathi language, which he did not know before, so that he could afterwards understand, read, write and speak it at will."

Irene Piper, only ten years old, could converse with the Chinese and invite them, in Chinese, to her church to accept salvation, all by the power of God alone. One man, May Lee, declared that "her accent was perfect; her forms of speech so exact that ten years study would not have given the average Occidental such knowledge of the language."

An American missionary, Miss Lillian Keys, of Peking, China, while employing a Chinese carpenter understood the questions he asked her about the work he was planning to do. She knew no Chinese, he no English, yet she understood all he said to her as easily as if he has been speaking in English. She answered in tongues, which turned out to be the Chinese. So they both understood each other; the carpentry work was completed, and the Lord was glorified.

Another person similarly used was Mable Smith-Hall, one of our early successful pioneer evangelists. Her father, a practicing physician, lived in Galveston, Texas where, from all over the world, foreign ships with their sailors docked.

When the group of Pentecostal workers would go to the street service each evening, in the crowds which gathered there were sure to be some of these visiting sailors. While she was preaching, her language would soon change from English into tongues. Sometimes she would preach almost the entire sermon in one foreign tongue; sometimes she would use perhaps as many as three or four. Always there was someone in the audience who would understood what she was saying, and after the service would want to talk with her in his native tongue. But as far as I ever know, she couldn't carry on a conversation with them as Mrs. Montgomery often did.

When the fullness of the Holy Ghost baptism is received, "believers" invariably "speak with other tongues as the Spirit gives them utterance"; but few people seem to receive the full "gift" of healing, the "gift" of working of miracles, or any other of the nine special "gifts."

This notwithstanding, all "believers" may scripturally lay hands on the sick and have them recover, apart from the "gifts" of healing-just as they may also speak in "other tongues" by the Spirits power when they are baptized by the Holy Ghost, without ever receiving the "gifts of tongues," or of speaking in various languages as Mrs. Montgomery did, and as others still do. Confusion reigns in the minds of some as to why "tongues" are any more important as evidence of the Baptism than some of the other gifts. I believe the main characteristic of Salvation, most often taken to be the evidence of the Holy Spirit Baptism, is great joy.

But "great joy" is Scripturally a result of a Salvation. All Christians-that is, active, praying, worshipping Christians, in contradistinction to church membership only-always have joy. A union with Christ brings that.

A true Christian without deep joy is momentarily under a cloud-a cloud of some kind, perhaps cares, worry, sickness, or doubt have hidden Him from their sight. In this sense, joy may be said to have a fluctuating quality. For this reason alone, it could not always be depended upon as evidence of the Baptism of the Holy Ghost.

Many emotions can produce joy. But beyond the power of joy, or of any other abstract quality to speak intelligently, instantaneously, perfectly, and fluently in a strange language, except when an intelligence greater than one's own has taken over.

Which is exactly what He does. And is the reason why it becomes His final evidence of the incoming of the Holy Spirit, and reveals the fact that this person is now under God's complete domination, having freely and entirely yielded body, soul and spirit to Him, as of now.

A simple illustration. When an ambassador on foreign soil moves into the official residence of his own country, his native flag is immediately flown aloft proclaiming his presence there, backed by his nations full authority to look after every phase of his country's interests.

So when a man yields himself to come fully to God's residence here on earth, the Holy Ghost takes up His abode in His new home, raises this miracle-standard of the Kingdom of God, to which the man now belongs, and stands fully ready by day or by night to further God's plans in this earth.

"Thy kingdom come! Thy will be done on earth as it is (done) in heaven."

It has been committed to only us-creatures of both time and Eternity-to bring this about. God has entrusted it to us. Let no man fall short of his privilege to glorify God.

"But he spoke of the temple of his body."
"Ye are the temple of God."

But the gift of love, it seems to me, is the most necessary accompaniment which the Spirit freely confers. The power to love God supremely, unselfishly, wholly; to lay down our lives day after day for others, as Jesus did, was graciously granted to us, along with the Baptism of the Holy Ghost, it being both a gift from God, and a fruit of the Spirit as well.

When the Lord chose to send this Latter Day revival, He first scattered it out in the open like manna, for all to partake freely.

But sad to say, many acted out Satan's same old script, deterred only by the existing civil laws, which a few Jewish leaders of Jesus' day had enacted long ago.

Thus they cut themselves and their followers off from the power and authority vested in the genuine attested Baptism of the Holy Ghost. But millions did go on to see signs, wonders and miracles in profusion; nor have these miracles ceased. They have been slowly but steadily increasing in such numbers and power that one is left almost breathless with amazement at the mighty acts of God in this earth. Thank God that I have lived to see this day!

# Chapter 12

God was pouring out His Spirit in other towns as well, for wherever we went He gave revivals.

A Camp Meeting was announced in Houston for August 1906. I went up early to help work on a Tabernacle which was being built on a lot given to us by my Brother and Sister M. E. Layne. It was located near their home in Brunner, a suburb of Houston, and was the first Pentecostal Tabernacle ever erected in the "Apostolic Faith Movement."

It was a good Camp and many people attended. Brothers Parham and Carrothers were in charge. The Lord blessed as usual. Brother and Sister O. P. Shirer, Sister M. E. Layne and many other neighbors opened their homes to the visitors. Sister Layne, who had three grown sons near my age, was like a mother to all the young workers. For years their consecrated means, gladly given, were a great help in spreading the Gospel. We appreciated all the more the sweet fellowship enjoyed in these homes and gatherings, since the Pentecostal Way was not an easy one in those days, and most of us in this Texas group were merely youngsters.

Fresh from the revival in Los Angeles, Sister Lucy Farrow returned to attend this Camp Meeting. Although colored, she was received as a messenger of the Lord to us, even in the Deep South of Texas.

One day she preached and told about the Great outpouring at Azusa Street. After she finished speaking, she prayed for the people to receive the Holy Ghost. The Lord had been using her to lay hands on the people and pray. God would then fill them with the Holy Ghost and speak through them in other tongues.

A long line of the people queued up before the platform, and as she laid her hands upon each head, one after the other received the baptism of the Holy Ghost, and she spoke in other tongues. But what interested me most was that everyone for whom she prayed was speaking in tongues.

When I saw this, my heart became hungry again for another manifestation of God. I had not spoken in tongues since my initial experience a few months previous. So I went forward that she might place her hands upon me. When she did, the Spirit of God again struck me like a bolt of lightning; the Power of God surged through my body, and I again began speaking in tongues.

From that day to this I have always been able to speak in tongues at any time I yielded to the Spirit of God. Since this ability is with me all the time, I try never to use it unless God specially leads.

I know what Paul means in the 14th Chapter of his letter to the Corinthian Church. I have thanked God for this experience all these years and for the power and privilege of speaking now in tongues at will. I thank God for Sister Lucy Farrow, who later went to Africa as a missionary, and still later, while in Africa, went home to glory.

Another blessing I received in the Houston Camp Meeting was when the brethren ordained me to the ministry. It was here also that the first definite Organization took place. Up to this time Brother Parham was called the "Founder and Projector of the Apostolic Faith Movement," and all alone he had issued credentials under that name. Brother Carrothers was now appointed General Field Director for the U.S.A. and I was appointed field Director of Texas.

The latter part of 1906 was spent traveling over the District, looking after the various meetings going on in the different cities and towns of the state. There were about sixty of our ministers and workers in the field at this time in Texas and my part was to help out wherever there was a special need.

# Chapter 13

Early in 1907, brother Carrothers and I decided to have a Convention and Short-Term Bible School for our workers at Waco. It was called for February, and most of our ministers came in from their stations to attend.

Several important ideas were being privately advanced, analyzed, and mulled over by the preachers. They were mostly points of doctrine, which really required a fair and open discussion, and a final public setting. Many new ministers of various faiths had received the Holy Ghost by now and had become part of the group.

Some still retained ideas which they had received "by tradition" from their former connections, but had not as yet been approved by the Holy Ghost in our midst. These doctrines had already been raising question on the field; such subjects, of necessity, were to come before this Convention for a final decision.

Daniel C. Opperman, having recently resigned as principal of the high school system of Zion City, Illinois, was attending this Convention and seeking the Baptism of the Holy Ghost. Because of ill health, he had come to Houston and had been instantly healed of tuberculosis when he obeyed God, and stepped out on the streets, preaching Christ to the passerby.

During this session in Waco, one of the subjects introduced was whether speaking in tongues was the initial evidence of the baptism of the Holy Ghost, or just another gift on par with all other Scriptural gifts. This idea, as I have said, had been recently introduced among us by some of the newcomers.

One or two of our new preachers took the orthodox position that any one of the nine gifts of the Spirit could be as much an evidence of the Holy Ghost baptism as could speaking in tongues.

Brother Carrothers and I led those who maintained that all would speak in tongues when they received the full baptism of the Holy Ghost, and that the nine gifts of 1 Cor. 12:8-11 were given to the believers after they had received the Holy Ghost. Interest ran high when we attempted to defend a doctrine which some doubted.

A day was finally chosen for an open discussion of the Scriptures on this subject. It was quite a session. Brother A. G. Canada led the opposition, and, as he was a gifted speaker, none of us could predict what the outcome would be. Brother Carrothers had been an attorney-at-law in Houston before entering the ministry. This training, with the Spiritual ability he also possessed, proved to be a great help in analyzing and "rightly" dividing the Word of Truth. As a conclusion to the prolonged Biblical discussion, he summed up the evidence of the Word of God by using as his clinching point the quotation: "For they heard them speak with tongues and magnify God."

As a climax, he showed that the connective "for" (or because) used in Acts 10:45-46 could not honestly be ignored, nor be lightly set aside.

He argued that this was the pivotal point of the narrative, confirming as it does, that the speaking in tongues alone finally convinced the Jews that the Gentiles as well as themselves had actually received the Holy Ghost.

We could see that God was mightily helping him to unfold wise and logical deductions and, as he closed his masterly discourse, God came down upon all of us in great power and blessing, confirming this teaching in each one of our hearts as never before. For most of us the question was settled once and for all. After almost fifty years, I still have not the slightest doubt whatsoever along this line.

This question never arose again in our ranks until years later, when Brother F. F. Bosworth, who had come amongst us, printed and circulated his little booklet, Do All Speak In Tongues? I believe the Assemblies of God at that time publicly reaffirmed their stand, as against his idea.

While attending the Camp Meeting during the previous summer, I had become engaged to Miss Millicent McClendon of Alvin, Texas, one of our most promising young lady evangelists. I left the Bible School on February 24th, 1907, and went to Alvin where we were married, and later returned to the school in Waco.

Most of the School met us at the railroad station and gave us a hearty welcome. After the greetings were over they put us at the head of the usual line of marching students, Millicent and I carrying aloft the large banner, "Apostolic Faith Movement" between us-a signal honor. We marched through the streets signing the songs of Zion, and after holding the regular evening street service returned to the Bible School.

When this School closed, a group of workers headed by A. G. Canada was sent to San Antonio with the Pentecostal message and there also a great revival broke out. Brother T. Matthew Bowen, later pastor for many years of one of the largest and most beautiful of our churches in Houston, was one of the workers in this revival, as well as D. C. O. Opperman and his wife, Hattie Allen.

As a further confirmation from the Lord of their decision as to tongues being the crowning Biblical evidence of the Baptism of the Holy Ghost, and for the sake of all those whose arguments had been defeated, this San Antonio group decided, before they left the School, to make the next meeting a test meeting.

We all knew that no one had ever before preached or taught tongues as an evidence of the Baptism in this new and faraway city. So they covenanted together that none of them would mention tongues, or an "evidence" in any way whatever in San Antonio. They prayed and committed the results to the Lord, preaching only the Baptism of the Spirit.

None of the citizens there had ever heard of it. These workers endeavored honestly in every way to give God a further chance to straighten them out if they were wrong in their conclusions, and thus to make it a fuller, fairer test. Therefore, no seeker was expecting any unusual manifestation. But it made no difference. They all likewise spoke in tongues as the Spirit gave utterance when they received the Holy Ghost. This satisfied even the most skeptical among us.

It was in this San Antonio revival that Brother Opperman received his baptism. Brother L. C. Hall, who at the time was a Christian and Missionary Alliance Pastor there, also received the Baptism after attending several of the meetings.

One day the workers heard Brother Hall praying and praising the Lord down in the tent where he had gone alone to pray. He had a powerful voice and he was using it mightily in praise and worship of the Lord. Of course, it stirred the whole neighborhood so that a great crowd gathered and, unknown to him, stood watching, while he received the Holy Ghost.

Thus after two hours of praising the Lord and without any assistance from anyone, he came gloriously through, baptized by the God who answers by fire, and began speaking in other tongues. Every seeker in that meeting did likewise. This permanently established the doctrine as a tenet of the new movement.

Brother Hall ministered to our Camp Meeting that following summer and henceforth became a great blessing to our work, and to us. For about forty years this noble character was a fearless, outspoken evangelist among us.

All that he was by birth, breeding, intellect and talents was humbly at the Master's disposal… and how God used him!!!

A successful soul-winner, he never failed to sweep his audience along with him, clinching every point, as he logically, sanely, Scripturally, powerfully tore them loose from old scriptural thought-patterns, and sent them out into the full stream of God's unchanging Word, will and work.

He had an usual gift of mimicry. Often, where words might have been resented, he got his idea happily across with a quick impish smile and a droll, expressive gesture which did the trick perfectly.

A profound thinker, his logic was irrefutable. Coupled with a ready wit and, upon occasion, an effective touch of sarcasm, his mimicry could so successfully point up pulpit pomposity or ostentation-his pet peeve-or any other insincerity which he needed to expose that an audience would shake with laughter. But he would go serenely and gravely on with his discourse. In this way he would accomplish in a moment what mere words perhaps could never have done.

He was a man of unusual personal distinction, of high principles, uncompromising and faithful. But he attacked only that which was contrary to the Word of God.

I have sometimes heard our leaders remind young preachers to be original, telling them above all not to try to copy "L. C.," for there was only one "L. C. Hall," and there never could be another. We call him "The Prince of Evangelists" because he had neither equal nor peer. An accomplished musician, he composed many deeply spiritual hymns which were much loved and appreciated.

A truly great soul, he since has gone to the city of God, but his work remains.

At this point, I would like to pay tribute to the character, zeal and consecration of all these early workers. They were truly the salt of the earth. Their consecration and sincerity was so deep that there was no room for anything other than God and His sweet will in their lives.

A Scriptural characteristic which all alike possessed, and one which invariable accompanied both the Early and the Latter Rain outpourings of the Holy Ghost, was a spirit of prevailing prayer and holy boldness. Prayer being of a private nature, this Scriptural boldness became an indisputable sign to the public, a sign that no one could quite explain away. This was one thing our opponents could not get around. Perhaps a lack of fear might describe this attitude more clearly. Later, as ministers, their grand imperturbability under stress, their complete composure, whether high or low, their courage in every kind of situation inspired confidence and trust, and made them leaders worthy to be followed.

As Verkuyl renders it: "As they observed the freedom of speech on the part of Peter and John and took it that they were men without schooling or skill, they marveled, and they recognized them as having been with Jesus. Besides looking at the man standing with them perfectly healed, they had nothing controversial to say."

Anyone who was convincible at all could find God in our meetings, for God revealed Himself in His glory to all those whose hearts were hungry for more of Him.

When platform-shy young boys and girls, as well as older people, would stand up among friends and acquaintances, sometimes with even antagonistic relatives present, and give a rousing testimony about things of God, they knew these people "had been with Jesus," for this could not possibly have been done without some tremendous assistance. It was astonishing what God did for many people in this way.

I remember one little ten-year old boy from the mountains, who had never seen a street car, nor electricity, nor even a rest-room, preach night after night under the power of the Spirit, while great crowds of sophisticated city people sat gasping in astonishment at the words which flowed from his lips. I heard many say, "He could not possibly know what he is saying!" This was true. His address was scholarly, his rhetoric flawless, his arguments and exposition profound. That God spoke through him, I never heard anyone doubt.

Again, some who later became top-flight executives in our work were as children, and so far as a knowledge of the world was concerned, not too far ahead of baby robins... children of the wild-children nature. But God saw their inherent ability, coupled with a great hunger for Himself, so He began their tutelage under the Holy Spirit which developed all their powers to the highest degree. When God calls an individual, He allows not only the exact work that he is to do, but for the preparation for that work as well.

One of the reasons that some educational centers are often harmful to young preachers is that certain teachers or instructors, like the proverbial bull in a china shop, lack the heavenly wisdom, the knowledge of things spiritual, to enable them to understand the delicate nuances of the Spirit of God. Unless they themselves are deeply consecrated, selfless, and teaching by the Spirit of God alone, they will surely do untold harm and little good. For such young ministers, life, which has promised so much, becomes a tragedy. Worst of all, they may never discover the cause of their failure, nor the reason for it.

One great stumbling block, however, to the naturally minded church member as well as to the teacher is the incomprehensible difference between the Scriptural "walking in the Spirit," and "walking in the flesh." "For as many as are led by the Spirit of God, they are the sons of God." Even the sinner who upholds virtue, honor and integrity has the reward within himself, as well a God's approbation on clean living. A highly moral man, apart from salvation entirely, sometimes lives such a life. But the sad part is that these at last are all alike without a Savior, and thus have no Scriptural promise of ever seeing Heaven, because they have not actually been adopted into

God's family, nor have they legally become his child and thereby have no rightful claim on Him.

We all strove to be great soul-winners, always attempting to pack "just one more" fish into the usually full Gospel net.
"Action" was our watchword. Jesus "went above" doing good.
Men of constant prayer and faith are usually men of accomplishment. In the beginning God made His pattern for preaching so uncomplicated that-given a willing mind-even a child could successfully follow it. For Scriptural preaching is entirely dependent for its power upon the Holy Spirit. Preaching, we felt, served mainly to hold the audience at attention while God mightily strove with them and deftly worked!
While we poured in the Holy Scriptures, heated on our part by prayer, by fasting, by self-denial, by consecrated, concentrated zeal, all unsuspected by the audience, God was so adroitly manipulating every heart and mind and every conscience that few people could ever be the same again after sitting through one service. God made grappling hooks of His Pentecostal preachers rather than bookworms.
Those who succumbed to being bookworms, those who did not enjoy the strenuous swimming which the full tide of God's rescue operations required, He gently steered toward quiet, shallow waters where we lost sight of them. They could be satisfied with less, so less they got! Why? Because books are in themselves only dead things. They cannot, apart from God, give life. Alone they are inactive, inoperative. A book is too still to generate life by itself.

Men who are in a dying condition need quick work-quick operations and great presence of mind on the part of the operator-if life is to be restored before it is too late.

Our ministers worked together like a life-saving crew, each manning his own station, or city, for God actively superintended those "led by the Spirit." (Rom. 8:14) Thus all Bible colleges have in it their power to turn out either bookworms or soul-winners, because there are primarily two predominant types of sermons, as well as men. One type attempts to produce a sermon which is a rare treat of intellectual perfection, flawlessly presented, designed mainly to be contemplated and enjoyed, much as a poem, a painting, or some other work of a great master is appreciated.

The other type of sermon may only be presenting the bare, naked truths of Scripture, but skillfully designed to produce the fervent activism of obedience, and start men toward God. As in all else, between these two extremes lies the middle ground where study and action are both used in suitable proportions as needed.

Early disciples, as well as those of later date, spoke with the authority of both a dynamic revelation of truth direct from God to their own hearts, and out of the fullness of their own soul's dramatic experiences with God... an unbeatable combination of dynamics at any age.

The formula for revivals with healings, miracles, signs and wonders following still is: be fully obedient to God and His Word yourself, then preach the Word until the Word takes hold.

Many of our most successful early workers had no formal training for the ministry. Their training was received on the field under the tutelage of the Holy Ghost as they went. But that was spiritually sufficient. Churches were established which stand today, soul-saving stations which are a monument to what God can accomplish through men who yield to Him. Neither these early pioneers, nor the humble beginnings of many of our large churches should be forgotten amid the great temporal and spiritual prosperity existing among us today.

But, sad to say, a few second-generation preachers are now being tempted to sow the seeds of careless living, to eat the bread of idleness, to neglect prayer and Bible reading, while apparently waiting for someone to drop a finished pastorate with its attendant revenue into their laps.

We had some of these in the early days, too, but the last I heard of most of them, they were still waiting. The trouble, at least with some, was that they did not recognize opportunity when they saw it.

Comforting is the thought that somewhere along its length, every busy street presents an opportunity and a challenge to step out and begin presenting the Gospel. Every city, town and suburb presents opportunities so numerous that the God-called and aggressive heart is always overwhelmed by the vastness of the white harvest field.

Although one's place may not be in full-time ministry, there are, however, hundreds of other places, important or not, depending upon how one looks at it, which need developing equally as much. Because one may not see an opportunity is no reason to become discouraged. One can find some other line of Christian activity and execute it with all one's heart and soul. To such I would say, God needs you, and will surely use and bless this service when presented to Him.

Many years ago, when calico was priced at five to ten cents per yard, a sixteen-year-old girl with only one calico dress to her name had received the Baptism of the Holy Ghost at Eureka Springs, Arkansas. She answered a distant call for cotton-pickers. While picking barefoot in the fields, she kept praying for, and witnessing to the "pickers" around her, intensely hoping they might find the Christ she had found. As there was no church of her faith nearby, some of her fellow workers secured the use of a schoolhouse for evening praying meetings. She testified and said to them of her experience as best she could. Some of her listeners became soundly converted and great revival started. When it became too big for her to handle, she sent for a minister to help her. He forged it into a good and prosperous Assembly. As I remember it, she had no call to preach, but she just did "what she could."

Occurrences similar to this happened over and over because all our people, wherever they went, either preached or testified to the Gospel, and God gave the increase. Woodrow Wilson once said truly, "It is enthusiasm that sets the powers free."

Whenever my wife and I went to a new town to preach the Baptism of the Holy Ghost to the people, we usually would get our audience with us enough to be sure they were listening. My wife, who was an evangelist, would say something like this: "I'm no prophet, so I cannot tell you how this meeting is going to turn out, but there is one thing I can be sure of: that is, that all the best Christians in the town will receive our message, also the baptism of the Holy Ghost, or He would not have sent us here." So we were entirely safe. It never failed.

"Nothing is hard to a willing mind." All success is dependent upon this fact. And we were willing to suffer; willing to go hungry; willing to be cold, uncomfortable, insecure; to take beatings, misrepresentations; to become the butt of jokes and pranks; to suffer losses; to be deprived of rest, of home, of loved ones; to be thrown on a cold and unfriendly world without money and often without a place to lay our heads; to accept joyfully any persecution or trouble the Lord allowed the Devil to stir up, while praying for the salvation of our tormentors, because we believed all the Bible, and in it was said "all things work together for the good to them that love the Lord, and are called according to His purpose." And we surely did love Him and were definitely called to His work.

This same difficulty is still found in the Mission field wherever a new work is being opened up. Only a few days ago a missionary said publicly that one of their converted native young men came to them and, while discussing the possibility of opening a station in a new district, said: "Well, I'm not worth much in a venture like this, but I'd be willing to go along and take the beating myself instead of you." Bless his heart! He had already learned from experience that he could take it. And so had we.

# Chapter 14

You may wonder about these evangelistic "Bands" mentioned before. They were an integral and vitally necessary part of evangelistic efforts. Physically, the most attractive feature of our work was the newness of young people all on fire for God.

An old saying, widely believed and fatalistically accepted, was: "young folks first sew their crop of wild oats before becoming Christians, in order to get it out of their systems." Consequently, very little attention was paid to youth at all. Naturally, everyone was greatly surprised when they first heard our young workers praising the Lord, "right out loud!... and not in church either!"

From the very first Pentecostal revival, God got the attention of the young people, and began calling out those whom He had chosen for leaders. Older leaders were chosen also, but the ratio was perhaps six to one. Joel's prophecy (Joel 1:21-32) was often used as a sermon text. Other passages in this end-time Latter Rain prophetic book were frequently used. The impact of their fulfillment before one's very eyes was terrific.

Then, too, we found that several deeply consecrated, vitally interested persons, consecrating heaven-propelled prayers on one locality, brought results. Rarely could one evangelist go into a new field alone and turn the community upside down for God in a short time. Jesus did not attempt it, far less then should we.

Years later, when we first arrived in Malvern, Arkansas, where over 250 were saved and baptized in the Holy Ghost during the first two months, the revival had started almost immediately. But we soon found that the way had been prepared before us by a sister upon whom God had poured out a travail for souls, after filling her with the Holy Ghost. For five year she had spent the greater part of every weekday travailing in intercessory prayer, pleading for her neighbors, acquaintances and the surrounding country. The answer to her prayers was indeed overwhelming. She had "done what she could."

All of us lived entirely by faith, and would have been thought by the workers to be hopelessly backslidden had anyone mentioned a salary, or suggested a certain sum as desirable. As we took the Scriptures literally, "Having food and raiment, let us be therewith content," we were full. The vast majority of us went gladly anywhere God sent us, leaving it entirely up to Him for the supplying of our needs. Sometimes it was only used clothing-perhaps a gift-but the heart of the giver was kind. Perhaps a garment was entirely unsuited to us, but we wore it thankfully, happy that we had achieved enough humility to do so. We literally proved the statement: "Godliness with contentment is great gain." Our only concern was that our lives, in every detail, be lived exactly to Bible pattern.

Consistently enough there had to be unity. Anyone who could not keep the unity of the Spirit with every other member of his band was either given a railroad ticket and sent home, or perhaps given another chance in a different band. But no disunity could be allowed. The power of God would not fall upon such a condition. We often saw it happen that when there was disagreement no one could be prayed through at the altar service. Meetings would be locked tight, finances would fail, and the heavens turn to brass.

Husband and wives sometimes failed through lack of harmony, accord, or unity with each other. Prayers would go unanswered until they acquired unity. Once all was clear, the heavens would open again, the power of God would fall upon the seekers once more, and all would be well. Whenever we struck a snag of any kind we fasted and prayed until it was removed. It could be said that this movement was born, grew and flourished on the Bible formula: obedience, faith, fasting, and prevailing prayer.

In one meeting the break in the revival had come and people were getting through to the Lord at the altar service night after night as fast as popping corn.

But on one occasion instead of the usual liberty, everything was bound. For three days no new converts came forward. No one prayed through. Liberty was gone. Everything was at a standstill. The leader and his wife examined their own hearts. As far as they knew, there was nothing wrong anywhere. The workers with them seemed to know of nothing. They knew the Lord was displeased, but where to find the trouble? They had to start fasting and praying to discover the hindrance.

On the third night as they neared home, the leader glimpsed two of the young workers, a girl and a boy, who had come home ahead of them, standing and talking under a light in the back hall. With the glimpse came the knowledge of what was wrong. He went in and asked them at once if they "were sweet on each other (the current expression then), and they confessed it. A harmless little flirtation we would call it today, but it successfully cut off God's power because they had not only broken their agreement, but were putting "self" first. Each worker who went out had to agree to the ruling: "no courting on the field." When anyone broke this agreement, they were automatically disqualified. God is a God of principle and honor. And they had voluntarily given their word, God had a right to expect them to live up to it.

After both young people had sought God's forgiveness, the boy was sent back to Headquarters the next day, and that night God's power came down again as before.

I might say here that only the highest form of lovemaking was allowed at any time. People whom God had joined together in the Spirit of marriage did not hinder a meeting at all. In revival (and we were in one most of the time) it could often be told which love affair had God's approval and which was only a flirtation by whether God honored it or not, in letting His power fall as usual.

To become a shirker, a deserter, or to be indolent was anathema. "No man, having put his hand to the plow, and looking back, is fit for the kingdom of God." (Luke 6:22) Anyone who deserted his post for any reason other than complete physical inability to carry on, was disgraced, and almost never found his place again in God's work. If they attempted a comeback, evidently something fundamental in themselves seemed to prevent them from succeeding permanently. Many easily discouraged people felt the call of God and over the years have gone into the work. But when the going got rough, or became monotonous – which it seldom was – they found excuses for themselves, and returned home, never to attempt the work again. Some lost touch with God entirely, and were thought of as failures for both time and eternity.

Now I have come to believe that God may call some for a special public duty during a certain period of time, and when the task is finished, their work done, they go back to take up their usual routine again. Such can be a great blessing to God's work.

For transportation, our workers rode in trains or horse-drawn carriages, if they could afford it. If not, they rode bicycles, or in lumber wagons; some went horseback, some walked. Often, they waded creeks. Often men removed their clothes, tied their bundles above their heads and swam rivers. How they got where God wanted them wasn't important. To be there: that was the thing!

The workers lived wherever a vacant place was open to them: in mansions, lovely residences, old hotels, in old stores, in abandoned buildings, in Negro rent houses, in covered wagons, gypsy-style, in shacks, in tents, or under any other kind of shelter.

In establishing new works, vacant residences were usually scarce. Sometimes they were non-existent. My wife and I finally learned that in almost every town there was one, if not more – supposed-to-be – "haunted houses." Most of them were in excellent condition. As a vacant house produced no revenue, the owners were always glad to let us have one for as long as we wished, rent free. Our occupancy always broke the spell of fear over the community and every haunted house we left became a good money-maker.

None of us had any furniture, as far as I can remember, that could rightfully be called furniture. It was rare that anything but discarded furnishings were ever given to us. I know we slept on every kind of bed: on wooden slats covered with a ticking filled with dried corn husks; on benches in the church after the crowd was gone; on the ground; on the floor; on tables, or on two or three chairs placed side by side; under trees – anywhere. The reason for this was that we went everywhere if we thought that there we would rescue a lost soul. If Jesus would have gone, we went. We always remembered that Jesus had no place to lay His head; that He slept in a stable, and so consider ourselves better off than He was.

We put up with bedbugs, flies, mosquitos, cockroaches, fleas and rats when it became necessary. In fact, we sometimes had suspicion that the devil sent these creatures along in droves to discourage us and send us home. But God often freed us from such plagues by a miracle.

Once in Joplin, Missouri, Hardy Mitchell and his wife arrived first to engage and prepare quarters for a short-term Bible School. Among other buildings, they rented two large three-story residences in good condition, and were surprised that such good buildings were vacant, and held at such low rentals. Even so, it was all they could afford, so they rejoiced and thanked God.

They rented furniture for both houses and chose their own room. That night as soon as the lights were out, an army of bedbugs began to march on them. The bugs came in droves out of walls, and from all parts of the room. Horrified, Brother and Sister Mitchell stayed up for several hours trying to evade them, since killing them seemed to be ineffectual. Useless also, since reinforcements quickly took the place of the dead ones. They were heart-sick! They had never thought of bugs! Their money was all gone and the workers would begin to arrive early the next morning. Finally, in sheer desperation, Brother Mitchell stood up, and in the name of the Lord, rebuked every bedbug in that house or in any other building he had rented, and commanded them to leave immediately. He told his wife it was now up to them to lie down quietly in faith and go to sleep. Believe it or not, sleep they did – undisturbed! A hundred or more people attended that school and not one trace of a bedbug was ever seen.

Hardy Mitchell was one evangelist, who, with only his wife accompanying him, could go into a new field and have a good revival started within a week's time. He was a tall, handsome, young man with crisp blond curls. He had calloused knees, so his wife said, from kneeling beside his bed in prayer. He really worked at praying. When we was not in meetings, she said he often spent eighteen hours a day talking with God. He was answered accordingly with signs and wonders, and several times raised the dead to life.

His wife, a lovely girl, played the organ for him, and never failed to kneel at the organ stool, praying silently, earnestly, effectively, while he preached. His altar service was usually a landslide.

With this God-given, nonetheless human, ability to sacrifice and endure hardships, neither the Pentecostal work at home or abroad, as it exists today, could have been possible. Many willing hands helped turn the wheels of the chariot when the going was heavy; strong backs everywhere helped when it was needed. It was and still is a tale of loving sacrifice gladly given. It called, to borrow a phrase, for "blood and sweat, and tears," but it brought far more happiness than tears, for the tears that hurt were only those shed in despair at our own weaknesses, or inabilities, or our lack of holy hearts. But the joy of enduring for Jesus' sake a little of what He endured for us and of "triumphing" everywhere so that Christ became "the odor of a sweet smell" was so great, so satisfying that nothing else could take its place. Truly, He made our lives "a constant pageant of triumph in Christ, diffusing the perfume of His knowledge everywhere" by us, and liberating despairing souls from Satan's bondage. How I thank God for the small part I was allowed to play in this great Last Day move of God and for all the great souls, both men and women, who played their part nobly and well, and who gladly and happily bore the brunt of the fighting.

There was, by common consent, little joking or teasing. But I believe this always happens I n times of stress or strain. Years after, when pressure had lightened, and our numbers had grown, we, too, could relax somewhat. By then we had many willing hands, heads and hearts to help us to carry the burden.

Perhaps the Early Church did the same thing. When lives are in danger, few people can relax enough to joke or tease. This has always been the norm, I think, for completely dedicated souls in any age.

Of course, many amusing things happened, which, when retold to the group, provoked a good laugh and managed momentarily to relax our seriousness.

The daily routine began with Bible Study and prayer each morning. Prayer used up spare moments during any hour, day or night.

We preached to people in factories each noon hour. House to house visitations filled the afternoons. Street meetings were conducted every night, as were the immediately following evening evangelistic services. Then came the after, or altar service of prayer and seeking God, which lasted until the last seeker had ceased praying. This could be anywhere from midnight to six o'clock the next morning. The girls usually stayed until the women seekers were gone. The boys remained with the men who were usually the last to leave. This altar service was the crowning climax to our day, the one in which we could really see all our labor and sacrifices bearing fruit.

Converts made in this way were a replica of ourselves-earnest, sincere, devoted. These were the most rewarding house which, I believe, ever came to any man or woman.

As individuals, we gathered up all our resources-scattered moments of time, used and unused talents, capabilities-and threw them all wisely, and with a glorious abandon, into God's work here on earth.

Since all sin, slight disobediences, procrastinations were gone, there was no friction within our beings, so we could see clearly, judge wisely, plan capably, and execute efficiently. Of course, we didn't realize this then, but looking back, and also judging by results, it seems so. We could follow the Lord's lead without hindrance. Be that as it may, when fused into a whole, each one of us slipped into and held the position where he was needed most, without jealousy, rivalry, envy, or without any other of the "works of the flesh" which never fail to hinder success.

Watching some of these bands synchronize with God, one was reminded spiritually of the mystical picture King Solomon drew of the Lord and His Church in one of his beautiful word paintings:

"Who is she that looketh forth as the morning, fair as the moon, clear as the sun, and terrible as an army with banners . . . thou art beautiful, O my love!"

No wonder the devil hated them, for in God's hands they were invincible, and wrought great destruction in Satan's ranks.

Of course, these bands were all conducted in the strictest possible manner. If there was a married couple in the band or an elderly woman, they usually acted as chaperons, becoming responsible to God and to the State Overseer for the conduct of us all.

"Neither said any of them that ought which he possessed was his own, but they had all things common." (Acts 4:43).

Home, friends, comfort, money… everything on earth was forgotten in the all-consuming desire for the salvation of lost souls, and for God's truth to be made known. Consequently, those who went into the work left everything behind.

The personal holiness, the purity of principle and motive demanded of each of us was so great, comparatively speaking, that many onlookers believed we were either insane over religion, or drunk on some glorious dream.

Sometimes we almost had to pinch ourselves to find out whether or not we could be dreaming, we were so gloriously changed.

But we knew only too well that our sins were gone! Disappeared! They were cast so far away we had even forgotten what they were like! And God had forgotten too.

But with us always-when we tried proving it to ourselves could analyze, of the bedrock fact of our constantly answered personal prayers.

Requests for everything-our health, our clothing, and our food, meal by meal-was routed through Heaven back to us. All of us kept well. A place to live, a place to preach, transportation problems, words with which to grip and move an audience toward God-all these things had the same routing and the same fulfillment.

# Chapter 15

After the Waco School closed, Millicent and I spent the spring of 1907 in opening a work in McGregor, Texas. We labored there for several weeks. Then the greatest test of our whole lives from Satan struck our movement through a terrible blow from within.

One of our leading ministers fell into an awful sin, which turned out to be only a temporary affair, as he repented, confessed, was forgiven, and afterward lived an exemplary life so far as I ever heard. However, this discouraged our Texas workers so that most of them left the field and went home. Our company remained with us at McGregor. After this happened, there were no more workers to oversee.

Since the system which had previously been setup to advance the work was dissolved, I resigned as field director. Under his leadership, many of the workers came back on the field and began to hold revivals. So, the work started forward again, but without any formal organization. L. C. Hall attended this Camp Meeting, which was his first after he had received the Baptism.

With the company of workers, we prepared to go to Austin, the capital of Texas, to open a work there. Dan and Rosa Caldwalder, and Walter Hall rounded out our band. When we were ready to leave for Austin, we found that we had no train fare. For several days the five of us prayed and waited on God to supply our need. Finally, the Lord touched Sister Katie Field's heart when she heard of it, and she supplied our fare.

Arriving in Austin, where no one had ever heard of this new movement, we had $1.35 among the five of us. The women sat in the depot all day while we went out to locate a place for our tent-an old tarpaulin which we had brought up with us from Houston.

After a brief search, I went to a residence to inquire about a vacant lot next door. I told the woman who answered the door that I wanted to put up a gospel tent in which to conduct a revival. As I turned to leave she called, "Will you please wait a moment?" She went into the house and returned with a five-dollar bill which she handed to me. No word of finances had been mentioned. Later on, in the day while inquiring about another lot in another section of the city, another woman gave me five dollars for expenses. Still a third five was given to me.

At a lumber yard a man gave me $2.50. When I returned to the depot, I had secured a lot, had lumber for seats, and despite having mentioned our need to no one, had $17.50 in cash left-a large sum in those days. We rented a residence and furniture the next day, put up a tent, seated it, and were ready for the revival.

The Lord truly sent people, for by this time many had heard of us and were curious to know about this new religion. At first, we were very disturbed by the antagonistic crowds around the tent. And also, by the persecution and opposition of some of the townspeople. Feelings ran high. The city police did not see fit to protect us or to enforce order. However, a unit of Texas Rangers was stationed a few blocks away, and when I was forced to appeal to them for help, they gave us adequate protection in true, old-time Texas Ranger style. We soon had a great revival at our hands.

Many of the best people of the town now attended the services and accepted the message. Although I doubt no account-as we never counted our converts-there must have been at least 150 to 200 filled with the Spirit, and many more healed and saved.

Millicent had started preaching about the same time I had received the Baptism, and God mightily used her as an evangelist, her special gift. Our workers called her "Little David" because of her remarkable preaching ability, her beautiful voice, and because one of her sermons was about the meeting of David and Goliath. God used her here in Austin as she did most of the night preaching.

Our tent was first located on East Twelfth Street. Then we held another meeting on East First Street. Later in the Fall we rented a hall uptown, and the revival still continued. When we were ready to leave Austin, we turned the work over to J. D. Shumack, while we went on to Snyder, Texas, to hold another revival.

Millicent had been to Snyder in a meeting before we were married, and God had given her outstanding success. From Snyder, Texas, we went North to my home church in Galena, Kansas, for a meeting. Sister Fannie Dobson was still pastor, and my dear mother was a member of the congregation. During the services, Mother received the Baptism of the Holy Spirit, and talked in tongues accompanied by laughter.

When I first left home to go into the ministry, my father told me never to darken his doors again. I went away thinking I would never again be welcomed into my father's house. But relayed this news to my father; I do not know. When I returned to Galena, I did not go to my father's home, but to the parsonage where my wife and I were to be entertained.

Soon Mother said to Father:

"We ought to have Howard and Millicent out to dinner some day.

"Shall we invite them on Sunday?"

To which he replied, "Yes, if you want them."

Whether he had forgotten what he had said previously, or whether he chose to overlook it, I never knew. He welcomed us in his usual quiet way and nothing was said. Several years later, he, himself, and one of his married sons were converted in a Methodist revival held in Galena, and were united with the church. Now almost the entire family are church people. Truly, we had a great time in the Lord during our stay there.

After that revival we were asked to go to Lucas, Iowa, to open a new work. We went there in February of 1908. It was rather cold for Millicent since she had been brought up only a few miles from the waters of the Gulf of Mexico. Several of the Texas workers were with us, including young Hardy Mitchell, the boy preacher, of Houston. He was a great help to us and, with my wife, both being evangelists, shared the night preaching. I taught the Bible in the afternoon services. Some of our prominent workers came into Pentecost during that meeting, Brother John Goben among them.

We went to Des Moines, then to Centerville, Iowa, for another revival, and by way of Galena back to Texas, working in and around Houston for a while.

In one of these northern places, we were invited to stay in a millionaire's house but he was so cheap that, although it mid-winter, he would not furnish adequate heat, but kept the house at about fifty degrees Fahrenheit, which was far too chilly for Southerners. Nor did we ever have a warm meal there. Nothing ever was put on the table but cold sliced beef and baker's bread. Nevertheless, we did our best to endure hardships as good soldiers, thankfully.

After this Camp, Brother E. J. Bayse, a Pentecostal business man who had formerly lived in Houston, but was now in Stuttgart, Arkansas, bought us a large, new Gospel Tent, and asked us to come to Arkansas to open up new fields there.

We used the tent in Stuttgart, Pine Bluff, Redfield, Hot Springs, Malvern and Benton. This tent became a real blessing to God's work, and the means of many, many people finding God, for He certainly wrought in that state at that time.

We invited Brother Frank Anderson of San Antonio, a young tinsmith, to assist us in some of these meetings. He left his business, came to us in Pine Bluff, Arkansas, and proved to be a great blessing in prayer and altar work. These two elements were the outward essentials upon which all our revivals were built.

Brother Frank tells a story which goes something like this: for some time, the Lord had been dealing with him to leave all things and enter the ministry. He had noticed, however, that many of the workers on the field had not been able to renew their original wardrobe once it had served its usefulness, so he hesitated.

He and his brother were getting a new business on its feet, and he was reluctant to leave it, just as it was beginning to pay well. In the meantime, he had purchased a large new trunk and had been laying away articles of clothing, some by the dozens of pairs, and some by the half dozens, until he had all he wanted. Finally, he began to add several new tailor-made suits to his array. He decided that now he had enough good clothing to keep them well dressed for several years to come. So, when the unexpected call came, he left his business to his brother and bought a few extra things to divide with other young preachers who were in need. Then he joined our band at Pine Bluff.

Before he arrived, we had rented a residence in which there was a rear lean-to room. This became Brother Frank's room and in it he neatly arranged all his possessions. The meeting was progressing nicely. There were teaching in the day services and evangelistic services at night. The crowds were coming, and on the whole, things were not nearly as bad as Brother Frank had expected them to be.

However, at the tent one night during the service, someone came and told the workers that our house was on fire. When Brother Frank arrived, he found that not only his room had caught fire, and all its contents had been destroyed before the fire-men could extinguish the flames. The clothes on his back were now his only possessions. He said he knew instantly why God had allowed this to happen. In trying to provide and insure himself against hardships of any kind, he had cut himself off from the privilege of knowing God's care and provision in times of need. He said he learned there and then never to try to insulate himself from God, and thus stunt his own spiritual growth, but always to trust God, who knew what was best. Later Brother Anderson became a successful pastor and evangelist and was much used of God in the gifts as well.

# Chapter 16

Since its inception the Pentecostal Way has never been an easy one, nor was it in our day. When anyone stepped out from the crowd or from the religious world, it was no wonder that they immediately became a target for the Enemy. Former pastors had preached, no doubt sincerely for so many years, that healing was not for present-day people; that it was only a special power given to the apostles to help establish the early, infant Church; that all gifts of any kind had "died" with the apostles, that the Church people all alike were thoroughly convinced that all this was true. So, for some unknown, unorthodox people, especially young people, to hear preaching that all this power was restored in Christ was so astounding and so unbelievable that the majority did not believe it, nor do many today.

But to claim to have been really baptized in the Holy Ghost, which the twelve Apostles were choice enough to receive, with Divine evidence sent down from Heaven itself, was to many, especially to God-fearing people, blasphemy.

Oftentimes people would be so aghast that they would ejaculate: "Why they must think they are better than God himself, for even Jesus did not have that experience!" Such was many a person's conception of a Bible they could not understand. Some did suggest that this might even be the sin against the Holy Ghost. But the Scriptures were so plain on the subject, and God so unmistakably "bore us witness with signs and wonders following." That after a few years of unintentional, nevertheless, intense persecution, all our gainsayers found that, no matter how wrong they may have thought we were, their persecution of us only fanned the flame.

God came to our defense whenever we sorely needed it; He protected and preserved us. They soon found that the traps they set for us sprang upon themselves. But many years passed in the interim.

Numerous are the instances which could be cited of persecutions suddenly stopped, of hindrances removed. Almost every town we opened up to this Gospel had similar instances of how God helped and delivered us. A few of these will suffice.

Brother Lyons, of Arlington, Texas, in telling of his conversion around 1906 said, as well as I remember, that he was driving a milk wagon at the time the Pentecostal meetings came to his town. His route lay past the Workers' residence. As it was level country and a small town, he could see the Workers' house and garden two or three blocks away, while he was making his rounds. Just as it would begin to grow light in the morning, he could see Millicent McClendon, the girl evangelist, walking up and down the garden path with her arms raised to heaven, praying. He was a sinner at the time, rough and wild of heart, and he said it infuriated him more and more each day, until he felt he could gladly kill all the band. A few other men seemed to feel the same as he did, so a crowd of them went to the tent one evening fully prepared to "run them out of town."

That night he stood with his gang outside the tent. The same little freckled-faced, red-headed girl evangelist mightily preached under the power of the Spirit. God took hold of Brother Lyons, and when the altar call was given, he fell at the altar, calling upon God for mercy. He later fond that the rest of the group were all there beside him praying and seeking God. Not too long after, he was preaching, and had many years of successful ministry before he was called Home.

Another time, much later, when we were trying to get a foothold for God's work in a city in Arkansas, a certain spot seemed to the workers to be the most suitable location, a spot God wanted them to have. But a woman real estate agent who jointly owned the property, blocked the way, and refused to sell. Finally, she said that she "would see them in ---- first." The next day an automobile in which she was riding turned over down a hillside. She was killed instantly, although no one else was even hurt. The deal went through. God had many souls in that city whom He proposed to save, heal, and fill with the Spirit, which He later did.

Many a man was converted while he was honestly trying to decide whether or not to help run the workers out of town. If the devil couldn't incite the people with one tale, he quickly circulated another. It seemed that it mattered not what, so long as souls were turned away from finding God. But he often overstepped himself and told something which drew the crowd instead of scattering it. Such was the "hypnotism" tale. It was frequently rumored that these men had the power to hypnotize people, put them through an altar service, and bring them out speaking in other tongues. Few at that time had ever seen a hypnotist, or knew his limitations, so curiously often brought great crowds.

When, as a young girl, my present wife first came to our services, it was through the tale. She had seen hypnotists give a few public demonstrations and felt quite sure she could tell by watching us whether we hypnotized people or not. She and her eldest brother came, and during the altar service, while several hundred seekers were praying, drew close where she would be sure to miss nothing. She decided at once there was no "hypnotic power" in Millicent, as she did not have the personality for it. She studied Brother Garrigher, but he was very fair, and appeared quite mild. Then, as Ethel did nothing by halves, they waited until I came near to speak to someone. When they saw my "small, yellow eyes," she and her brother left. Recounting her opinion of it to him, disparagingly and inelegantly, she said of me: "As for him, he couldn't hypnotize a cat!"

But we could never be sure we were not going to be injured. Some workers had been attacked, some had been beaten, some had bones broken, some were jailed, some were made to leave town, some were rotten-egged and some where shot at. We were stoned, but at least we were never "sawn asunder." Church services were disturbed by roughnecks for many years. Tents, buildings and sometimes residences were burned: drinking water was poisoned, windows were broken. We were sometimes threatened by angry mobs or by raging individuals when some member of their family had been converted. Often, we had no protection; there were times when the police chose to close their eyes because we were the strangers, while the city paid them a salary.

But the most perplexing and annoying thing of all was that almost always, in a first revival, the devil sent in some people to attend a few services, who would temporarily seem to lose their minds during the service, and had to have several strong men to hold them still. God usually handled this disturbance by causing some leading, level-headed cracker-barrel authority to say dryly, "Well, they didn't have far to go. This might have happened anywhere they went." Which was true. This usually removed that reproach for us, and quieted public talk.

We privately knew, however, that Satan had been forced-bound by the body of this person-to come nearer to us than he enjoyed, and that he was responding in Biblical New Testament fashion. We always saw that the Satan-sent person got home safely. After a day or so of prayer for them, they were always all right.

The hardest thing of all, though, is to see one of your own young converts driven out of his mind by Satan. But, fortunately, this rarely happens.

Aside from some basic physical weakness, we usually found, after talking with them later, that they had spiritually left some open gate of disobedience, some chink in their spiritual armor through which Satan could attack them. The fact that they had deliberately sinned and thus left the protection of the Blood of Christ was hazardous enough. But when they refused before God to make their wrongs right, Satan began to play up his advantage. This, coupled with an accusing conscience-the result was disastrous.

God could not protect them because they were Christians who had started behind Satan's battle line, and would be held there until they repented and called on God for restoration.

But there is always unlimited safety for the upright soul in Christ.

Suffering was characteristic of aggressive Gospel work in Jesus' day, and it still is! The devil is just as much alive as he was in Jesus' time. But so is God!

"Who makes a way of escape that we may be able to bear it." We bore it all because of our passion for the salvation of souls.

It was sometimes the case that a young worker was not satisfied, or felt that he had not worn his spurs spiritually until he had at least a few stones, a few tomatoes or rotten oranges thrown at him or at his tent, for Jesus sake. We knew that if we couldn't make that much impression on Satan's territory, something was wrong. I have seen workers exultant over persecution, feeling that they had arrived, counting it joy to serve under him, and so share a bit of His reproach.

Few of us had dreams of world conquest. God was truly our captain. He alone knew what He was doing, and we were quite willing to have it so. That He was forging the great movement which now covers the earth never entered most of our minds. We had no ambition for anything except to be like Jesus and more useful to Him. All our attention and time were given to the job immediately at hand. There was never any time to rest, nor to count spoils, nor even to appreciate fully what God had already done. We were all intent upon the job of the moment.

# Chapter 17

The type of conversions God was giving were so deep and powerful, so pungent and overwhelming, that people's lives were drastically changed from midnight into midday, one might safely say. Where people had been shy, backward and timid before, they now were bold and adventurous for the Lord Jesus. Their rousing testimonies and their fervent witnessing's carried God's message deep into all hearts. Some yielded to God; some resisted His Spirit, but they all had their chance.

Some could at once see and recognize the presence of God and contact Him. A few scoffed or derided, according to their natures.

Many people seemed to think of this movement as being some new, competitive doctrine which a group of young irresponsible had recently hatched and certainly not as the "good news" of the Gospel, the "tidings of great joy" which God long ago had sent through the Lord Jesus to all races and colors, nations and denominations.

We, however, who had been fortunate enough to have eaten and drunk at His table, were so deliciously happy and overflowing with satisfaction that we could talk of little else. The field was ours. Working hard, we hoped to see the wholly worked saved.

Because of these things tension at times ran quite high. Our opponents, mostly out of fear of the unusual-I think-a few, perhaps, jealous of the crowds, would sometimes attempt to incite the public against us.

Some Southern churches in which the spiritual tide was low had, prior to this, brought reproach on

Churches in general because they had been allowed to become filled with dead timber, as it were. Godly standards had been lowered until almost any sinner could easily join the church and be received with open arms. In fact, sinners were often enthusiastically compelled to join such a church because some members thought they would "fit in."

This practice was thought to be entirely Scriptural, because did not the Bible say, "God into the highways and byways"... which must mean sinners, they reasoned... "and compel them to come in"?

Many accepted from the hand of God what He was offering. Some were indifferent. A few considered us only a personal affront to themselves.

Some congregations in this way ordinarily had less than a dozen people who gave any sign of being Christians. They tell me that in certain sections some were so cold or paralyzed scripturally that no one dared say "Amen" or "Praise the Lord" aloud in service, even if they wanted to, for fear of disturbing the speaker. A few speakers would become so annoyed at such interruption that they would immediately turn and sit down. Others, more patient, would announce that if the disturbance was repeated, they would stop "until the ushers had cleared the building, and this misguided person had been ejected."

One woman, who five years before we came had been filled with the Spirit but didn't know what to make of it, had been asked to leave every church in the town in which she lived, and not to return, simply because she would say "Amen" two or three times during a service. She was soon not allowed to attend any place of worship on the grounds that she was a "disturber of the peace." Did not the Bible say, "Let all things be done decently and in order?" Saying "Amen" was out of order in their church, they told her.

This church, as an emergency measure, announced a business meeting each Wednesday night for as long as our revival might last, in order to withdraw fellowship from those who had received the Baptism of the Holy Ghost during the past week. I heard that during the first few weeks they had released forty memberships. But these have mostly all made good Pentecostalists so we profited.

When asked why anyone would object to people getting more of God, they were told that these people were all becoming demon possessed just as people had in Jesus day.

To this the people replied, "But we have been taught the possession by the demonic power ceased during the Apostle's day. How does it happen that it is now suddenly being resurrected?" But Jehovah, who is a promoter, "plants His footsteps on the sea," and "rides upon the storm." What might frighten us would not disturb Him at all. According to the Psalmist, He might even greatly enjoy a little praise and thanksgiving in His House.

I remember that one Sunday night in the Ozark Mountains, (while my wife was preaching an evangelistic sermon under heavy anointing), some disturbers threw a few stones and fired several shots simultaneously through the windows of the church, one round passing directly before her face. However she was so absorbed in the message God was giving out through her that she noticed nothing wrong until the audience automatically bowed over and completely disappeared among the seats.

My first reaction, when I heard it, was to duck my head behind the top of the old church organ, for I, too, had been brought up in frontier country. With the next thought, I realized that Ethel was standing up there alone and unprotected. Immediately I stood beside her, between her and one of the windows from which the firing had come. She had not even heard the stones nor the shots. Aware that she suddenly had no audience, she stopped, spoke to me softly and asked, "what happened?"

Again, when reactionists attended our meetings, it was difficult for them to understand why we had public altar services.

The most progressive of the denominational churches had gladly limited their evangelistic efforts to a two-week revival each summer. Then they imported an evangelist to "put it over." The preaching and advice was excellent, designed to get action and they usually had several additions to the church. It was all done very decorously and properly for fear someone might-just get "emotional." Throughout, they maintained what they honestly believed to be an attitude of worship. The congregation felt pretty cramped, but they, too, hoped they were worshipping. If anyone became God-conscious of their sins, enough to weep or pray, they were much more immediately conscious of each other. How the news would fly the next day that they had been publicly obstreperous. If one must shed tears, it should be done with dignity and with as much distinction as one can achieve. Actually, it was more like setting out a batch of new bread, and then sitting on the cover to keep the yeast from working. Or like setting eggs under a hen for days and when they began to hatch, binding the eggs so tightly that the chick never got through. Many souls would like to have found God, but they were never led, nor encouraged, to go any further than conviction. Consequently, few ever really "prayed through" or touched God as in our altar services. They got deep conviction from the preaching but, as most of their leaders had only contempt for the old-fashioned "mourners bench," they had no one to guide them through to God, and the seekers themselves soon became afraid and stopped praying, just short of making live contact with God.

They wrongly concluded, therefore, that conviction was the only "joy and peace" to be found in salvation. So, upon invitation, they could afterwards conscientiously join the church, believing that religion had been overrated, over-emphasized and over-preached. But such liberty at this was only for a certain two weeks in each year. As soon as it was over, everyone was expected to return to normalcy at once. But if one died, or fell ill in between those times, it was merely a streak of bad luck for you.

But God changed all that. He took a parent strain of people who had experienced a conversion like Paul's "old things passed away, and behold all things are become new"- bound them together and set them working for him. As a result, our prayer services were our main feature. We were not afraid of God, nor of what He might do. Hence, these services were not held secretly, nor behind closed doors. We knew we had nothing to be ashamed of, nor to apologize for, for we cared only for God's opinion, and for His will to be done here, and now and everywhere.

Kneeling at an altar mainly served to hold people still before God, while they were encouraged, even assisted, to pray, confess, repent, believe, receive, and make direct contact with God.

Stranger still was it that these people, who were so reactionary where God and His interests were concerned, prided themselves on being among the most progressive when it came to worldly interests – science, sports, the arts, business, or education – and pursued them with ardor and enthusiasm. The Christian's greatest loyalty, I still believe, should be to Christ, and His highest joy should be derived from serving Him.

# Chapter 18

Sometimes manifestations now began to appear which were not of God. A special empowerment from Heaven was needed at that time to sort out the doubtful from the Scriptural ones. Some we let run for a while in order to see what kind of fruit they bore, trying faithfully and impartially to keep only those which seemed to glorify God the most.

One striking demonstration of the Spirit was new and strange to everyone. Perplexing even to us at first, it was entirely Scriptural when properly conducted. This was the seekers falling under the power of God. We soon found that many such seekers had been through a heavenly experience, and we unaware that they had fallen. Anyways, there was seemingly no way we could curb it, for they were out like a light before we knew it, and nothing brought them to. Oblivious to everything, they kept worshipping the Lord.

We soon decided it was of God, as it most usually occurred in an altar service during prayer. Like things contacting a heavily charged electrified wire, they "fell at His feet as one dead!" We remembered that even the Apostle Paul had fallen to the ground and lay prone in the dusty road when Jesus appeared to him. God often came to seekers in such overwhelming power and glory that receptive humanity could scarcely retain its equilibrium while yielding to God.

God often uses simple measures, when necessary; to protect us from what might have become a tumult. Once I did not know just how things might turn out because a prominent and beautiful young church woman, one of many, had lain prostrate under the power of God for several hours, while she received the

Baptism of the Holy Ghost. This was too much for some, and even few tried to incite the public to violence.

A local wit, a man who had often molded public opinion by a droll remark, said of them: "Well, one thing's for sure; there's none of them got enough religion to fall under, even if they wanted to." This set the public laughing and order was restored. An occurrence like this often helped our work considerably.

This phenomenon alone was distinguishing enough to bring thousands to watch and "wonder." We soon saw that the prophecy of Habukkuk 1:15 was being fulfilled before our startled eyes:

"Behold ye among the heathen, and regard, and wonder marvelously;

for I will work a work in your day which ye shall not believe, though it

be told you."

Paul, while preaching in Antioch, quoted this scripture to his Jewish brethren:

"Beware therefore, lest that come upon you, which is spoken of in the prophets:

Behold ye despisers! –and wonder! – and perish! For I (Jehovah) work a

work in your days, a work which ye shall in no wise believe, though a man

declare it unto you!"

(Acts 13:40-41)

This was undoubtedly spoken by Paul to people whom he hoped to see accept the Baptism of the Holy Ghost, but who would not. Our leaders informed us that the manifestation mentioned above had been quite a common occurrence in the past during all great spiritual revivals. It is recorded as having happened often in John Wesley's work, as well as in the work of many others.

Some people didn't like it of course, but that was nothing. Some people didn't like God himself. We bowed to His will and let Him work as He chose.

To some, these manifestations marked our meetings as undesirable, of course, yet they most successfully advertised them as well. But we did not care a picayune for insignificant man's judgment or praise in such matters. God came first! How could humanity direct Him or set His limits, when we didn't even know what He was planning to accomplish? The Holy Spirit only knows fully the mind of God. Nor did we place supreme confidence in sermon construction, grammar, English or delivery. All of this savored of personal ambition. Had He not baptized us into the Holy Ghost in order for Him to speak through us to this generation?

No compromise with the Scriptures was made solely to please human ideas. God Himself was sufficient and versatile enough, when the pure Gospel was presented by the power of the Spirit, to meet all men on their own educational levels, and thus transform their lives.

"For Christ sent me…" says Paul, "to preach the Gospel not with wisdom of
    words" –mere words- "lest the Cross of Christ be invalidated!" -1 Cor 1:17

Of the Corinth revival, he explains further:
    "And my speech and my preaching was not with enticing words of man's wisdom,

but in demonstration of the Spirit and the power; that your faith should not stand
in the wisdom of men, but in the power of God." -1 Cor. 2:4-5

I agree that much of this is in the past and, of itself, scarcely worth recounting. But in a full and true picture of these early days and its influence on the movement as it shaped itself, every angle has its proportionate place because, at the time, it yielded a particular influence.

Brought up in Christianity, my wife used to often say she could not possibly understand why the Church at large did not accept the real Baptism of the Holy Ghost, enter into it, and make it their own. It was the logical thing to do. And the Church could have done it as easily as did we. She had the same God, the same Bible, the same privileges, the same promises.

How she could have possibly cut herself off from such a Heavenly bargain was hard to understand.

The Lord had baptized my wife in the Holy Ghost about six months before we arrived in her town, nor had she ever heard that there was a Pentecostal Movement or experience. She became hungry for God, sought him alone in her room, and He mightily filled her.

Why, as a whole the Church allowed us to grab off the ball, run with it, and win, world-wide, was a constant source of wonder to her.

Church history could have been re-written had she-the church-done so… But, in spite of all that:

Our hearts rejoiced on dancing feet; Our souls took wings and soared!

# Chapter 19

After Pine Bluff, we went to Texarkana for a short meeting, then back to Houston for a Convention announced for the Christmas holidays in Brunner Tabernacle. Erected near the Tabernacle, a large tent was used as a kitchen and dining room where meals were served on the free-will offering plan. This was another unusual feature of our work. All meals, beds, and rooms were given free to all who came. No charge was ever made for anything. We prayed for our supplies, God sent them in, and all shared alike.

Nor were the ministers who led the Camp or Convention paid either. They had "all things common," just as the others did. Always there was enough that came into the treasury to see all the workers and preachers to their next field of labor, to pay all bills, and to send home any visitor who might be stranded. Most visitors took care of themselves, and helped pay for the Camp as well.

It must be remembered that all that time poverty was the rule, not the exception.

This Convention unexpectedly continued past the holiday season and finally closed four months later.

Brother Carrothers was now the Houston Pastor. Many of the new ministers who had recently come into the work, and who later became leaders, attended this meeting. I met Brother E. N. Bell here for the first time and liked him very much. L. C. Hall, Daniel Opperman, A. P. Collins, Frank Bartleman and many other noted workers visited the Conference from time to time. God so transplanted these pastors, and later many others, into our midst that they became one of us, and pillars in the house of God in their own right.

This School became a powerhouse, God's transmitting station-call it Convention, revival, Bible School or what you will. It became all of these and more. My, how the Spirit, such as tongues, interpretation of tongues, prophesy, discerning of spirits, and the gifts of healing.

I could never tell all that took place during this time. One night I saw the Lord come upon Brother Frank Anderson and bestow upon him the real gift of interpretation of tongues. After that, he was used of the Lord in this kind of work in a special way for many years. Also, through the gift of prophecy, the Lord spoke to us just as He spoke to Barnabas and Paul! (Acts 13:1-7) Many times He spoke, revealing the secrets of men's hearts right out before the public, especially the secrets of us who had done things which had displeased the Holy Ghost. Not wicked things-we were far from that-but trivial things about which He wanted to have us teaching.

For example: I had charge of baptizing the converts and there were many of them. We had to walk half a mile from the Tabernacle to White Oak Bayou, I, wearing my baptismal garments. There was someone to be baptized almost every day. It was winter weather in the South; sometimes it was freezing, sometimes it was cold and raw. My clothes rarely had a chance to dry between one baptizing to the next. I murmured this matter over in my heart and wondered why some of the converts could not wait for a few days so that a great number could be baptized together.

During the next service, when I had just led the first candidate into the water and had turned around facing the great crowds of people gathered on the bank, the Lord began speaking to me through a message in tongues. I paused to listen. Then through the interpreter, He told me of the murmur I had voiced in secret of my own heart, and told me to confess it before the crowd, which I did. Then He went on talking to me, telling me of many other secret things which no one beside myself had known; He reproved me and admonished me, and after He had finished, He told me to raise my hands and praise Him. This I was glad to do, because I felt deeply honored and grateful to have had the Lord speak so directly to me. I have never since complained about baptizing anyone, even if my clothing never became warm or dry.

Another instance: two young men who were strangers to us came into our midst. One of them came from a far Northern state but both of them were preparing to become ministers. The first time they attended a day service they took a front seat. During the service, before the entire assembled School, they were called upon by name, and commanded by the Holy Spirit to stand up. At first, they hesitated, but when a stern rebuke came again commanding them to "Stand up!" they finally arose and stood before the Lord. Then the Lord began to talk to them.

The Northern boy had purchased a "Western Home Seekers Excursion" ticket, sold by the railroad which had brought him there, a ticket which did not include dining car meals, although a higher priced ticket did. This young man had gone into the diner with the higher priced class of excursionists and, undetected, had eaten meals during the entire trip for which he had not paid.

When God reminded him publicly of this, he tried to evade by saying that he had thought the meals were included. Sternly the Lord corrected him, "No! I told you on the train that you were doing wrong," and called upon him to confess the truth and seek forgiveness. Sorrowfully he did, and lived an exemplary life from then on, as far as I ever knew.

The other young man was next dealt with. He had boarded a train, had eluded the conductor and had traveled 350 miles without paying his fare at all. The Lord told him that he did not approve of stealing from a corporation anymore than from an individual. Both boys were finally told to repent and make restitution, which they did.

Some will no doubt wonder why God did not respect human dignity more than to humble these young ministers thus before us all.

We all truly wanted God's best. Human dignity can lend no glory to the majesty of God. Ministerial pomposity can never enhance God. As his representative, a clean heart does. Even a proud look He hates, while only a humble heart can be His home.

Again a lesson privately learned necessitates no public reproof later. To ride roughshod over the Spirit's secret reproof, as the two strangers had done, necessitated stern measures, if these young men were ever to become true men of God.

Here we also learned the difference between the Holy Ghost Himself operating this gift of the spirit, and the operating of it by our own spirit. Paul mentioned this when he said, "My spirit prayeth." Supporting this is the authority given the leaders, or prophets, who "sat by" to "judge" by which spirit they spoke (1 Cor. 14:14), thus deciding which was of greater or lesser importance.

Perhaps it might be interesting to enlarge upon this. We were taught that we could either speak from our own sanctified spirit, having the same value as preaching, or we could speak from the mouth of the Lord Himself. The usual speaking in tongues for messages as in 1 Cor. 14 Chapter is from out of one's own sanctified spirit acted upon by the Holy Ghost.

Sometime later a certain band had some teaching by tongues and interpretation given them in a message. Some of them accepted it, and some did not. I was not present at the time and knew nothing of it. This teaching was to the effect that God would forsake any and all Christians who ate any pork whatsoever.

Others who heard it had already been instructed according to the Scriptures in much the same way as we believe today. When the message was mentioned, they paid little attention to it. A short time after this happened, some of these same workers were in a new town, beginning a series of services. It was the first time my wife had ever preached for a revival. It so happened that at this particular place a gift of pork was brought to the workers' home during one of our food shortages, and as no one else seemed interested, rather than waste all of it, she ate what she could, although she rarely ever ate it for health's sake. Neither did she know that such a message had been given. The members of the band told her later that they fully expected to see God forsake her at any moment. But when, instead, He came mightily upon her each night in greater power and unction than ever before, they felt the Lord was sending them absolute proof that the message regarding abstinence from pork had been wrong and unscriptural.

While all this was going on in the home, a mighty revival broke out in the town and the nightly meetings ran for four months with hundreds of people converted, baptized in water, and filled with the Spirit. The messenger who had spoken about the pork tabu had guided the message slightly, perhaps semi-consciously, so that it would fit in with this own idea of non-pork-eating, which I believe many held at that time. Or perhaps instead of guiding the message, he had continued talking after the Lord had finished speaking, but while the anointing still lingered. This practice also accounts for many mistakes.

We all make, and have made, mistakes with the gifts, even the very best workers among us, and he was the best one of us at that time in our group. Even so, this should not be a matter of surprise. We were venturing out into new and untried paths, and there was no precedent, neither written nor spoken, except the Bible, to guide us in the actual operation of the gifts. Of course, most of these messages were Heaven-sent, as time proved.

But God will not be poured into any mould, no matter how fascinating to us, nor will He be at our beck and call as our personal wishes might sometimes highhandedly dictate. He uses His gifts just as a man uses his garden tools when gardening or leaves them unused when he chooses.

His gifts were never meant to take the place of either the Spirit of God or the Word of God, but to be used only as the "Spirit gives utterance." Thus, running ahead of the Spirit is most dangerous, because both speaker and hearer are without the protection of the Blood of Christ.

One present day winter comments: "The Prophet, in Scripture, is the mouthpiece or spokesman of God. He may speak of the past, the present, or the future. Prediction is incidental, not essential to prophecy.

"The gifts were given for mutual edification, not for entertainment or vain display. Misuse of the gifts of languages was a clean sign of the childishness of the Corinthians, for they were eager to display possession of the gift without any regard for the edification of others.

"Prophecy also was to be exercised within bounds. It was not to be like the turbulent, unrestrained ranting of the oracles of the false gods to which they were accustomed, whose spirits were beyond their control; but peaceful, discriminating discourse, two or three succession, yet ready to yield to another who may receive a revelation.

"Yet," This writer goes on to comment, "before the canon was complete, it was needful for the saints to have some means of knowing the mind of God. The Scriptures fully meet that need now."

To me it seems unlikely that the Lord would have bothered to give His Church gifts which were to become either impracticable, unnecessary, or obsolete. It isn't like Him to do so.

I would say that there is still use for the gifts, for both prophecy and for interpretation of tongues, for he who speaks, speaks not only for "edification" but for the present, personal, exhortation and comfort of the saints as well, although not safely for direction. Direction seems safest when guided by the still, small voice of God within the individual. However, when God wishes to speak in any other way, there is nothing we can do but accept it, and profit by it.

Years ago, we inquired after the welfare of a small, moneyless city Assembly which we knew lay in the Ohio River basin on low ground, in the pathway of one for its recent, most destructive floods. They told us that messages of both prophecy and tongues had come to the Assembly telling them that all of them were to evacuate the downtown district of their city on a certain given day. They obeyed, and later this date was found to be three days before the unexpected, oncoming flood. Through faith and obedience, not one of the saints suffered.

Now "we see through a glass darkly," instead of most clearly, as we like to think we do. So at best, we are yet only practicing, a fact which it is safest to admit. That God can accomplish anything at all through beings such as we, is a source of wonder, and should be the occasion for great praise and rejoicing.

There were in those days and still are people who try to operate spiritual gifts in unrighteous lives, but they are spurious. They are only the devil's counterfeits. They can never be of God:

"If we say that we have fellowship with him, and walk in darkness,
we lie and do not speak the truth: And hereby we do know that we
know Him, if we keep his commandments. He that saith, I know him
and keepeth not his commandments is a liar, and the truth is not in him."
1 John 1:16, 1 John, 2:3-4

We found, too, that a life of complete holiness and entire consecration was the only life God would accept and honor by His unfailing presence. As we all loved Him supremely, had forsaken all to win His favor and held not our very lives dear except for His sake, our companionship with Him was educative, abundantly sweet, and satisfying well.

This Houston Conference was a rigid school of training for our ministers and we thankfully received everything we obtained there. At the close of the gathering, I was asked to stay in Houston and look after the work in the city and to edit the paper which we published called The Apostolic Faith.

Before we were married, and while she was still a young worker, my wife attended a Bible School which was directed entirely by the gifts of the Spirit. There were some 86 students and all direction and teachings were by tongues and interpretation, or by prophecy. This school was on the highest level of the administration of the gifts she had ever seen, but it did not in every instance work out right. Even marriages were made by such directions. Of two so-directed marriages in this School, one turned out all right, but the other couple soon divorced. This kind of message was then on the upswing. While marrying fever, if I might call it that, was at its height, a public message came to this young lady, worded so ambiguously that many present, believed it meant that she was to marry a young minster also attending the School. She refused to consider it, saying that it was nothing meant for her. They became insistent that she was resisting the Holy Ghost. Reluctantly, she finally told them that God had previously completely settled her mind as to who she was to marry, if she were to marry at all. Then they left her alone. But no public acknowledgement was every made of the mistaken message. Somebody just spoke out of his own heart, ('my spirit prayeth') and not from God.

As I have said, on the whole, there was far more good than harm done in these Schools, a fact which we couldn't forget.

> "He that is down need fear no fall
> He that is low-no pride,
> He that is humble ever shall
> Have God to be His guide."

God sometimes spoke to us in an ordination service for ministers, but rarely to an individual among us. In fact, I never happened to have heard anyone so singled out.

Humility and fundamental honesty are great spiritual safeguards.

In some churches now the laying on of hands and prophesied over, seems to constitute full membership. Some seekers are, by this means, unknowingly shunted into a false position before the world. Often the secret desire of the leaders is only to enmesh the fish which they hope had been caught, and to boast of the increase in their following. This is a wrong motive and unworthy of true Christian character. Boasters, Biblically, are not found in the Christian category. It is a lack of such fundamental honestly and Christian love and consideration as this that makes me wary of some people's gifts. How often have such pastors allowed their own gifts, or the gifts of others to be used to shear his sheep, rather than to feed them; to give a false impression, rather than one of truth. This has turned many honest leaders away from making a place for the gifts at all, when these gifts might all have been used quietly, and to the advantage of God's people under proper circumstances.

I have often tried to help men whom I saw in danger. Some of them could see that they were weakening their own consciences, some could not. Nevertheless, the soul is on dangerous territory when we are unduly exploiting anything, even though we may excuse ourselves on the plea that it is to serve a good purpose.

Some dear saints, I'm afraid, will eventually wind up in sin as a result of giving gifts undue prominence. Some have already done this in years past and will again. To use a gift in its proper place in God's work, as a man would use an axe, a hammer, a saw, is right, but it is not spectacular enough for some. Neither will it always satisfy the people. When gifts have been advertised and used as a drawing card, people come to see and hear, and may not continue to return if nothing unusual happens. A preacher must almost be made of stone to keep an audience waiting in spite of such desire, until God's time when God really wishes to speak to a certain individual or congregation. Trapped, he may fake a message. Saul's sin was of the same nature when, unauthorized, he "forced" himself to offer sacrifices in a similar situation. Not many of the present-day interpretations and prophecy are directly from the mouth of God, but in importance, are on the level of the "spirit of testimony," (Rev 12:17, 19:10) and of about the same value as preaching or testifying. It is often an emanation from the spirit of prophecy but may not be true prophecy itself. That is, if it happens to be 100% God-operated. The Spirit of God upon one should be used safely and wisely, and none but the very humble and sincere of heart are honest and courageous enough to do so.

If I could do it humbly, I would say that we have not been as dumb all these years as we might have appeared. We, too, have seen all the tiny angles and places where we could have taken advantage of the public, where we could perhaps have been as revolutionary or spectacular as some who later failed. But rather, we made what we felt was the paramount consecration-to be deeply, sincerely honest before God, and with His people (Isa. 34:10). And this we have endeavored to be, even though we were-and always have been by some-thought of as prosaic.

In those days when the gifts of the Spirit were being so freely bestowed upon us, some even went too far, and a few imagined and even insisted that upon their arrival at their field of labor missionaries would receive the native language necessary to their missionary activities as a gift from the Lord, without the arduous toil of study.

Some prospective Missionaries went out expecting this to happen. When it did not happen, some were discouraged, and because of other unexpected disappointments left the field and returned home as quickly as possible. Others realized their mistake, allowed for it, plunged into hard work, and in spite of all misinformation, made good on the field.

As none of them had received the "gift" of tongues, they later all had to study to master the languages of their adopted country.

If we try to operate the gifts of the Spirit on the level of the works on the flesh, or of the natural minded man, we shall eventually fail, perhaps in some other test, seemingly unrelated to the gifts at all. One cannot drop out of the Spirit at any point and still be spiritually safe. Only repentance and restitution can restore us.

A young minister in Texas had prayed through to complete victory even over temptation. A member of her Assembly, the mother of several children and wife of an unsaved husband, had fallen and was quite seriously injured. Another member who lived next door, sensed the need, and sent over her fourteen-year-old Christian daughter to do the housework, during the time the injured woman was confined to her bed.

The unsaved husband succeeded in ruining this young girl. Soon the girl went violently insane. When the church members went to pray for her, she violently attacked them, and single-handed, drove them each from her room. No one could manage her at all. Finally, the lady minister after completing nine days of fasting with prayer went to visit her.

The insane girl made no attempt whatsoever to touch her, nor would she utter a word. Several times the worker visited her, but never was she attacked.

Finally, there came an opening in the crowded mental hospital nearby, and the girl was sent there. Six months later or so she returned home in her right mind.

The cured girl went immediately to visit this worker and confessed the entire unexpected and astonishing story. "But why did you not attack me?" the worker finally asked her. The young girl replied: "Because I could attack only those who were not entirely under the protection of the blood of Jesus. Perhaps they had not yet stopped yielding to impatience, criticism, doubts, fears or other imperfections. When they came into the room, I could see that their unprotected spots had the mastery over them. But the Blood covered you completely; there was no sin, so I was powerless. But all the time God was telling me that if I would confess to you and let you pray for me, He would heal me."

To keep honest, clean, and pure before God even in the most trivial things constitutes holiness of life and heart, and is essential to the victorious Christian life, and as assurance of companionship with God throughout eternity.

# Chapter 20

Homesickness often disqualified a worker. Everyone was so much under the burden for their particular meeting that they carried the burden for the salvation of souls night and day.

I was told of one lady worker who had an open tin box for a pin tray instead of the china saucer or small dish in which most of the women kept their pins. Since the tin box was not in key with her general appearance (she was the society matron type), one of the workers offered her a china saucer. She refused it. She said that when her editor-husband died, he had left her their beautiful two-story home and an ample personal income for life, while the bulk of his money went to their two sons who were in business. She had everything in the home her heart could wish, but she closed it up when she had an opportunity to go away to meetings. To keep herself in the necessary frame of mind for what we all endured, she never even allowed herself a piece of china, a dresser scarf, or anything that would remind her of home and thus through homesickness would draw her heart away from the Lord, or from His work.

The Lord's work in those days was not child's play, neither was it self-amusement. Wherever we happened to meet, whether in each other's homes or elsewhere, and whether there was a minister present or not, there was prayer, Bible-reading or singing. But almost without fail, there was prayer. Those baptized in the Holy Ghost lived in this atmosphere as naturally as fish live in water. Hence there was almost no teasing or joking, no relating of amusing anecdotes. There was little ordinary visiting among the preachers, or the saints either for that matter. We were looking for Jesus only, and we found Him! Praise His precious name!

As to order in our services, only a disturbance, which the Spirit Himself made, was tolerated. Each of us fully realized and were taught that the eternal fate of some soul depended upon our personal conduct, our staying under the blood, and in close contact with God every moment of our lives. We constantly walked in the Spirit. The devil quickly made trouble for anyone who was not completely clothed in God's armor.

Quietness, attention, and reverence were characteristic of the meetings. Anything else was quickly checked. Sometimes, in a new field, a stranger which especially appealed to him, but handclapping was quietly suppressed. We knew the tone of the service would immediately drop out of the Spirit to a natural level because God did not honor any mechanical worship into which even sinners could enter if they wished without deep heart worship. As clapping is purely a demonstration of self-expression, we had no time to waste upon it. Our business was to express Christ to the people, not to enjoy, or amuse ourselves, nor to receive the applause of men.

You might ask: were you able to keep a congregation growing and gathering momentum at such a high level? I would say: yes. I think the reason was, perhaps, that everyone who joined us had to suffer the loss of all things, as well as to endure persecutions. Therefore it took no amusements to entertain them, nor to keep them coming. When God worked, we had no trouble holding the crowds. God at work was the biggest attraction of all.

I well remember that the only kind of dancing we allowed then was allowed purely in the Spirit before the Lord. But it was truly before the Lord, and not before an audience. If the dancer's purposes became mixed or diluted, we started a song. Getting out of the Spirit was almost always handled by singing, at the time. Later friendly instruction was given privately. All public demonstration had to be entirely in the Spirit, as outsiders were quick to detect *self* and were quite vocal in pointing it out.

My wife says that the first public dancing in the Spirit which she had ever seen occurred in one of her own meetings long after she began preaching.

A young girl of seventeen or so, who was widely liked and respected in the community, and whose parents were Holiness in doctrine, lay prostrate under the power of God while she received the Baptism and finally spoke in tongues.

Almost immediately after, with eyes closed, she sat up unaided and reached out her hands toward Heaven with her hands still clasped. The gentle otherworldliness of the Spirit was still upon her. Her father sat watching, his tears streaming.

Her brother, a young Holiness minister who sat by, rose, took her hands and assisted her to her feet. With her eyes still closed, she turned slightly away from him, took a step forward, and with her face as much like an angelic being as I ever hope to see, began gently, quietly, rhythmically to dance before the Lord.

No sound had been uttered by any one of us for perhaps half an hour. God was so present in the room that to have spoken would have been a desecration.

All attention was focused upon her as the Spirit of God animated her as electricity might vitalize a robot.

Strong men cried. Tears were on almost every face. Tears and reverence. Rough men crept in from outside, drawn by this invisible Power. An outlaw, who had been drawn to a front seat, shook, trembled and wept. When it was over and the girl had quietly opened her eyes and slipped into her father's arms, this outlaw stood up and said to some of our Christian men, "Well, I never hope to see anything nearer Heaven than that! Nor get any nearer to an angel." After this manifestation, we had no more persecutions in that town.

An exhibition of "flesh" or of the forward human spirit, unsanctified by God, even though it might have been through "good people", is often revolting to people of intelligence. But I have never seen dancing that was God that did not touch someone in the audience.

Public dancing in certain services, as a practice, was later drawn from the colored work, where their freedom from inhibition, one of their most attractive traits, made its appeal. However, even there, it was always entirely controlled by the pastor, and stopped or started at his signal. As does any other pastor, he knew his congregation, no doubt, and allowed only what he considered beneficial. But this was a practice that had no place among us previously. Nevertheless, they had some mighty demonstrations of the Spirit among them at times and a solemnizing effect they had, too, even upon the wickedest.

Once in a large tent meeting, around 1912, a native African minister who had come preaching to this country was being featured at a large tent meeting in the colored district. His gifts were so outstanding that great crowds were in attendance. One night after the

138

singing had begun, he entered the tent, went straight to the platform and knelt in prayer, with his back to the waiting audience. He soon began praying aloud for two specific people who were present in the audience that night and who were committing a special sin which had been dealt with by a pastor in the city that day.

He prayed with tenderness and great pity for these two, and finally the Lord through prophecy, began to speak to them Himself, pointing out the different places where they had made the wrong choices. Then God dealt with the disgrace they had brought upon themselves, upon their distant families, and upon the work of God in general.

People who were present said that even the idlers around the tent, and the more vicious ones from the fringes of the dark, gathered silently and stood solidly packed around the tent, seeming scarcely to breathe. "You could have heard a pin drop," was the report.

This minister, still kneeling in prayer, also told them that their own one-whited-garments had become so covered with pin-point dots of wrong reasoning and practice that their white robes had now turned to a grimy gray. Having allowed so many of these tiny wrongs in their lives, they were soon following a dirty gray Spirit instead of the dazzlingly white purity of Christ. This substitute spirit had led them into the sin in which they now found themselves.

Finally, this evangelist began to tell them, while still kneeling, what to do to make their wrongs right.

He could not have heard, nor could he have found out in any other way, except through God, what their past had been, nor even that they were in the meeting for the first time that night. They were white workers out on their own...and I was the pastor who had dealt with them that day. It was truly God.

Finally, the minister rose from his knees and stood at the alter bench, and with his eyes still closed, called on them to come present themselves before the Lord for prayer, repentance and forgiveness. With breaking hearts they both came forward. Laying a hand on each head, he prayed so compassionately for them that the great audience fell to sobbing with them. They were finally directed to come back to me and to ask forgiveness. They were a chastened couple next day-sorry, humiliated and ashamed-when I gave them their train fare to their respective towns.

Many such uncovering God gave us in those early days when He lived among us as a Father, and it never failed to bear the peaceful fruits of righteousness and to put the fear of God, and the fear of wrongdoing into our hearts.

Perhaps you may wonder by what method the different companies or bands of workers and preachers were moved about in those days. We always depended upon the Lord to show us whether to go or stay, and to lead us individually. For our work and our service, each one of us was primarily answerable only to God.

As our membership grew, there was a fellowship amongst us, a love which supported each other in prayer and by advice, but to our own Master we stood or fell. Spirit-filled people were swift to detect any falling away.

There was usually only one preacher in each band while salary he was likely to get at any certain place was considered to be on his way out spiritually. When God said "Go," like good soldiers we went, asking no questions. Jesus never asked how much money He would receive for conducting a meeting-no more did we.

I remember well years, later, when I first heard that one of our preachers had demanded a guarantee of a fixed sum of money before he would consent to hold an evangelistic meeting, how astonished and sorrowful we all were. God had given him great ability to preach, but now he had stooped to sell his God-given gifts for gold! He wanted to use his gifts as a medium for bargaining! Our hearts were heavy.

When we talked to him about it, he said that some of the large churches had become so stingy they were withholding tithes to the hurt of their souls-which was really true-as well as causing the minister and his family unnecessary suffering-suffering which God had not intended them to go through. All this could not be denied. So one evil seemed to bring about another.

But the vast majority of us went gladly anywhere God sent us, leaving entirely to Him the supplying of our needs.

# Chapter 21

In the summer of 1909 we went back to Arkansas to hold meetings. We preached in Hot Springs, Stuttgart, and at a Camp meeting in Redfield. Here I was much pressed in the Spirit of God, also depressed in my own spirit, because of certain conditions in the meeting, which could not be surmounted.

One night after service, I went into the woods to pray and seek the Lord. While there, the Lord told me to "get up and go into a place which I will show you." After praying, I went to my room and told Millicent that we were leaving. Although we had no cash on hand, we began to pack, knowing that the Lord would supply our needs. He led us to Malvern, Arkansas, where we got a room in a hotel.

Next day I walked across the tracks to the first building toward town. I saw that it was a saloon. Standing in the door was an intelligent-looking business man, a type not usually found in a place like that, although the place was exceptionally neat and clean. He was quite approachable. After a few minutes' conversation, I asked him if there were any vacant lots near the center of town which could be secured for a tent revival. He mentioned one or two; then I asked him if there were rooms which could be rented for my wife and me. He told me that he and his wife lived in a big house alone, and that the upstairs floor had been made into a furnished apartment, the only one in town, although they had never yet rented it to anyone. He said that they would be glad to have us come to live with them. I went back to the hotel and told my wife. We both felt that this was the will of God for us.

While I was looking over the vacant lots in town, the Spirit spoke to me and said, "This is the place to put your tent."

I found that it was owned by a small Episcopal congregation who had erected no building as yet, but had purchased it for a church site. I easily obtained this tent ground, took Millicent to the lovely home where we were to live and where we launched the Malvern Campaign.

Because we had been persecuted so much by the Devil in other places, we decided to say nothing of who or what we were in Malvern, do no advertising, and get in our work for God before the Devil himself knew we were in town. Brother Carriger came to help us, and the Lord surely did work. Hundreds were converted, healed, and filled with the Spirit before the Enemy could find any ground for stirring up trouble against us. When he did, he arose in fury, but God had already worked ahead of him by giving us favor with the townspeople. These were the greatest meetings of my life up to that time. This revival ran for about three months in the tent, with souls getting through to God constantly, with many miraculous healings and conversions, too. An exhilarating red-hot revival!

Winter was near so we bought a lot, built a large Tabernacle, paid for it before it was finished, moved in and continued the revival there. Today there is a large brick Pentecostal church on that same site.

The Malvern Revival was outstanding in ministerial timber. Out of that one revival alone, the Lord called about seventy-five men and women to the field, many of whom are still active ministers. It was God working with us in such supernatural power that it convinced people that He was "not dead, nor gone on a journey," as we had imagined He might be, but was astonishingly alive, at work in His church, and could be contacted by faith and obedience.

Trying to tell how God worked in all of these meetings which I held, would be beyond the scope of this book. Beyond its scope, too, would be to tell of even a part of the sick, blind, crippled, deaf, who were healed over the years; of all the miraculous things God did when we needed it; of how He "confirmed the Word with signs following"; of the many thousands who were saved and filled with the Holy Ghost according to Acts 2:4; of the hundreds who were called to the ministry. In fact, there were few meetings where God did not work in His own special way in Latter Rain power.

One thing that made all this possible on my part was my health for which I must thank God. Since I was saved at nineteen years of age, I have never taken a holiday from shepherding, under God, the Church of His love. I never needed a rest or holiday from my labors which were also my joys.

I could always see that such a burden was too much for me to bear alone. I endeavored to do my best, and let Christ bear the rest for me. My nerves, if I have any, are perfect. At least nothing disturbs or annoys me enough to keep me from dropping asleep anywhere or anytime it is convenient. I have stayed awake for a week when it was necessary. Too, I could somehow see that I was to cooperate with the Lord and His Word, and do as He directed. Consequently, I've enjoyed every minute of my work for Him, and at seventy years of age am still enjoying it immensely.

Thank God for what He had done for all of us in the past. It is not, however, what we have accomplished which should concern any of us now. The question that should concern us is: shall we be ready when He comes for us with our work all done? We thank Him for all those who were able to bear the heat and burden of the day, for the "night cometh" all too soon in which no man can work.

# Chapter 22

Soon we began to feel the call of the Lord for evangelistic work again and invited Brother E. M. Bell as pastor for the large Malvern work. Brother Bell, before receiving his baptism and call into the Pentecostal work, had been the pastor of a Baptist church in Fort Worth, Texas. He was a bachelor of about forty-five years of age who had recently married a Pentecostal wife, a lady from Fort Worth, Texas. They moved to Malvern and took up their work there. For many years their home became our home and our headquarters as well. Brother Bell and I were close friends in the Lord and shared the burdens of the work together.

A paper called *The Word and Witness* had been sporadically issued at Houston, then in Fort Worth, at first under the name *The Apostolic Faith.* Now we published it in Malvern after Brother Bell had accepted the editorship in 1910.

Millicent and I went north to conduct a meeting in Des Moines, Iowa. After several weeks we were with Brother W. H. Durham in the old North Avenue Mission in Chicago, conducting a campaign.

Brother Bell later told me that when he became hungry for the Holy Ghost in his life, he had taken a year's leave of absence from his pastorate for the express purpose of going to the Durham Mission in Chicago, where he would stay before the Lord until he was "endued" with power from on high. As his church was also hungry, they began special prayer sessions during his absence.

He sought the Lord for eleven months there before God finally filled him. A graduate of the University of

Florida, the Baptist Seminary at Louisville, Kentucky, and with postgraduate work at the University of Chicago. He found he had to begin to read the Bible anew, as a little child might, and attempt to study it again as God would reveal His thoughts to him.

First, he spent eight days in fasting and prayer so that God would blot from his mind everything he had learned of which God did not wholly approve. He then began reading the Bible on his knees before God, and was amazed at the many really important points he had missed before.

When he finally returned home, quite a few members of his church had also received the Baptism. However, still following the call of the Lord, he resigned this pastorate in order to attend our Camp Meetings and Bible Schools.

Brother Bell was a man of good judgment, great wisdom, deep spirituality, and became a blessing to all. I remember him telling me of Brother Durham's Mission. The work among the Persians began there. Brother Andrew Urshan, whom I met for the first time, and several of his friends were students at the Moody Bible Institute when they first began seeking the Holy Ghost infilling. As they had no private place close by where they could pray aloud, they would walk way out on the ice of Lake Michigan, form a circle to protect them in some measure from the wind, kneel down and seek the Lord to their heart's content. I saw a snapshot not long ago of their group kneeling in prayer, with nothing in sight but ice and distance. They kept this up for many months.

Of course, it made a lot of noise, but who cared? In Heaven (Rev. 19:6) we knew there would be praises like "the voice of a great multitude"; "the voice of many water," and "the voice of mighty thundering" all praising God and saying, "Hallelujah! Amen!" So, each of us decided that we had just as well become accustomed to such praised, especially since the Holy Spirit Himself was instigating it. Who were *we* that we should refuse *Him*?

Another surprising feature of our work generally was this same vociferous, concerted prayer, and, indeed, it was truly vociferous! A tremendous surging life had been awakened within all of our spirits, at times almost beyond our power to control. The heavenly escape valve the Spirit gave us was prayer, praise, and worship.

When the power of God got to building up within us, it soon reached the level where vent had to be given to these floodtides of joy. We all knew, before we were converted, how we would have handled exuberant joy. But the Lord solved our problem in the right way. At every opportunity it was instinctive to drop to one's knees and start praying and praising. All the pent-up strength of body and soul was poured out and consumed by a tremendous wave of prayer, of praise and worship, which had enough spiritual momentum behind it to climb through Satan's opposing forces and immediately reach the throne of God.

I've sometimes watched an altar service in which saints were unselfishly laboring in prayer and travail, not for themselves, but for others, and I thought how safely and simply God steadied and solved young people's problems as well.

We were indeed filled with power and love, and like sunshine on gasoline, we easily expanded and ran over. Some had objected to the noise, of course, but the majority didn't mind.

These Persian students were members of Brother Durham's church, along with Aimee Semple, later McPherson, who had just returned from Hong Kong after losing her missionary husband, Robert Semple, in China.

Brother Bell said that this Mission was so full of the power of God while he was there that often a thick haze filled the top third of the Auditorium, like blue smoke in appearance. When this haze was present, people entering the church would sometimes fall in the aisles under the power of God even before they could reach their seats. People came through to the Baptism or to Divine healing around the clock.

Miracles of healing took place all the time. One night Mrs. Semple was carried in with a badly broken foot. When prayer was offered, it was instantly healed, and she walked out on her own power, without physical aid.

From the North Avenue Mission, we went to the Stone Church, pastored by Brother Piper. Before leaving Chicago, we visited Brother Sinclair's church. After two weeks meeting in old "No.9" in Indianapolis, and several weeks in St. Louis, we took a leisurely steamboat passage down the Mississippi River to Memphis.

We spent three wonderful days and night on the boat. They served the very best of meals and charged only $4.50 per person for the trip. What a pleasant time we had! How much we enjoyed that rest!

At Memphis, we held a few days meeting for Brother L. P. Adams, and after stopping at Stuttgart and Little Rock, we returned to Brother Bell's home in Malvern. Brother Bell and I had planned a Camp

Meeting at Malvern for that summer, so I took a trip around the state in the interest of the general work and the coming Camp. After my return, I stayed with Millicent until our little daughter was born. A few days later, Millicent passed away. It was an awful blow to me as well as to the work in general, since she was a powerful evangelist and had been a great blessing to many thousands of people. It was with a sad, heavy heart that I boarded the train with our baby, Gloria, and returned to Alvin, Texas, for her funeral which was held in the home of Millicent's parents. Many, many people mourned her passing.

Fortunately, the Camp Meeting at Malvern was soon coming up and it was my responsibility, as well as Brother Bell's, since he was new to the work in that state. Getting under the burden of the Camp Meeting helped me to get over the shock of my loss.

God gave us a wonderful meeting with over a hundred people filled with the Spirit in a period of ten days.

To get people to find the "door" into the Spirit realm, as Jesus said, was the hardest job we had. A report that so many were being filled with the Holy Ghost assured everyone that God had really been there in power. People were healed in every service and between times. Everywhere one stopped a worker and said, "Please pray for my healing." People were happy over miracles of healing, but little was thought about it. Perhaps they forgot to mention it again. If there were enough to form one line or three, they did, and whoever was near came and prayed for them.

Healing was taught as incidental to salvation, especially the Holy Ghost Baptism. "Of course, God would heal people!" we thought, and if they got right with God, and believed Him, healing would naturally follow. Without special prayer being offered, miracles often took place, just as a by-product of seeking God. Everyone who needed and really wanted healing got it- miracle or not.

Many leaders came for this Camp. There were Brothers Canada and Jackson who at that time worked together as an evangelistic tram; S. D. Kinne of St. Louis, who did a large part of the day teaching; D. C. O. Opperman, and Brother Durham from Chicago who also helped with the preaching. These and many others gathered from other centers to help with the Camp. As there were so many ministers in attendance, and all interested, the "Finished work of Calvary" vs. "The second Work of Grace" was officially discussed. In the controversy that ensued, as I watched both sides impartially, I soon saw that the doctrine of the "Finished work of Calvary" was right. It seemed that God opened my eyes to see that the Plan of Salvation was truly finished on the Cross and became ours just as fast as we could appropriate it all. So, for me the "Second Work" theory soon faded out. Our first Arkansas Camp came to a glorious close after having proved a blessing to thousands from all over the country.

From there we took the tent to Benton, Arkansas, a town near Malvern. We put it up, but it was soon cut down. We put it up again, but it was again cut down, and this time it was soaked with gasoline and was burned. The persecution was extreme.

Brother and Sister Philip Stokely were with us at this meeting. However, we quickly secured a building and after a long, hard siege, and the help and co-operation of several other workers, the Benton work was finally well established.

In Benton we heard that Brother Opperman and his assistants, Frank Anderson and Joe Roselli, were to open a short-term Bible School at Joplin, Missouri, that coming winter. Several of these schools had been held in various places and were a blessing to many of the saints and workers.

Brother Opperman's work among us was these short-term Bible Schools. Sometimes he acted as pastor, but teaching seemed to be his special gift. He would announce a school by faith, fully expecting God to meet every need, whether five came or five hundred. Assisting him were Hoe Roselli, of Houston, Texas, whom God used as a messenger, that is, he spoke the God-given message in tongues, which Frank Anderson would interpret. This messenger had a big responsibility. When he gave out a message in tongues he was completely in the Spirit himself, for it was possible for him to speak from out of his own spirit a message God did not send for that time. Even the interpreter, translating correctly, could not make it into the right message for that occasion.

Of course, these were tricky waters, but Brother Opperman was so "at attention" in the Spirit himself that every dangerous shoal or current was successfully navigated. If there were any casualties, I never heard of them.

He trained and put hundreds of workers into the Pentecostal harvest field. His schools were a "cutting out" station also, where those not called to active evangelism could painlessly find it out without regrets. These were safely channeled into other lines of God's service. For many years he was a handsome and commanding figure amongst us, full of faith and of the Holy Ghost.

He sometimes beautifully sang his experience in the words of the song:

"He's real to me! He's real to me
My father God is real to me!
My soul demands reality-
My father God is real to me!"

# Chapter 23

And the singing!

It was generally not the conventional church-hymn singing of that era. Entirely unpretentious, there appeared to be neither poetry nor musicianship in their composition. But there was something far more effective than either.

It could have been most aptly described, I think, Scripturally as a "joyful sound," since nothing pertaining to it prevented the "joy of the Lord" from seeping through.

The very artlessness of these songs, their apparent commonplaceness created no barriers of antagonism, but rather threw one off guard. After all, the hungry soul of man craved joy more than musicianship.

Previous to 1900, and up until Pentecostal singing appeared, there had usually been a distinct difference in the public mind between "worldly" and sacred music. But it was impossible for people freshly filled with the Holy Ghost to express their abounding joy in the slow, cold, reserved style typical of "sacred" music. Although we all sang at almost break-neck speed, we didn't notice the accelerated tempo. Anyway, everyone was jubilantly dancing inside, whether it showed outwardly or not. Being full of the Holy Ghost, we required a strong curb on the reins, much as a race horse ready to run must be held in. The fast singing style was really another of God's safety valves in our work, as well as a chance to shout His praises.

We were the first, so far as I know, to introduce this accelerated temp into Gospel singing. Fast music was then considered far too worldly for purposes of worship. Only those lacking in reverence were supposed to sing or enjoy lively music. Slow, dragging and listless, much of the approved church music of that day was irksome, to say the least, to the young in heart. When seeking amusement, young people went everywhere but to church. Consequently, entire towns would often have in them only one or two young people who tried to be Christians. Religion was openly said to be "only for old women and children." But God changed all that.

Simple, basic melodies, propelled by joyous voices, coupled with plain Scriptural wording, stamped tremendous and easily remembered truths upon every investigative mind, about almost every phase of religion and the Christian life.

"Blessed is the people who know that joyful sound;
they shall walk, O Lord, in the light of thy countenance."

These were truly blest and walked "in the light of His countenance."

"Jazzed-up hymns" they were sometimes designated by the critical, because this joy of the Lord was so built up in our young people that when they got a chance to sing, they exploded. Every particle of their being was poured into worship as they sang, nothing slowed them down, nor did their leaders attempt to curb them.

This crescendo of joyous, happy people singing unto the Lord was infectious. The sound of victorious Christian living wrapped you round. Unperceived, it seemed to slip down gently into the deeps of your affections, to tap at your heart's door, and unsuspected, to spread warmly through your entire being.

You had at first, no doubt, decided that such a desecration of church music was a disgrace to staid and ordinary Christianity. But soon something stirred within which caused you to reach for a book and lift your voice with the rest.

People who had never attempted to sing before felt free to sing along with us. Some could not manage a tune, but they could accompany us without fear of being conspicuous.

The young had at last found a mode of expression which matched their own high spirits, and the tug of life within them. They accepted it without question.

But a true musician soon found that he had been missing something contained in supposedly low-level church music that he had never before realized existed. Something potent! Something that had dynamic energy! That delivered the goods! All because God and His Word was in it! Here are a few titles:

*Trust and Obey. Where He leads I'll Follow. I Am Determined To Hold Out.*
*I'm To The Highlands Bound. Room For Jesus. Look To the Lamb of God.*
*Humble The Self To Walk With God. Hold To God's Unchanging Hand.*
*Be In Time, Sinner, Be In Time. When Our Lord Shall Come Again.*
*He Took My Sins Away. I've Anchored In Jesus. When The Saints Come Marching In.*
*The Healing Waters. I Would Not Be Denied. When I See The Blood.*
*O This Is Like heaven To Me. I'm On My Way To Heaven.*

*The Son Hath Made Me Free. Lift Him Up. Glory Hallelujah In My Soul.*
*Sin Can Never Enter There. I'm Going Through. One Of Them.*
*Where Shall I Be? Hallelujah, We Shall Rise. I've Received An Invitation.*
*Hide You In The Blood. Victory Ahead! Victory Ahead! Waiting On The Lord.*
*The Great Physician Now Is Near. Our Lord Is Coming Back To Earth Again.*
*He's Coming Again. Old Time Power. Not Ashamed Of Jesus.*
*Jesus The Light Of The World. The Meeting In The Air.*

Each one of these bore a distinct and definite Scriptural message, truths little known or suspected by the average church member. They contained great lessons and taught us all how to live. The things of the world, stripped of their glitter and show, were painlessly shown up for what they starkly were. No wonder these hymns brought conviction.

There were no solos, nor specials, as we know them now, unless Spirit prompted at the moment, for the message the song carried.

Such music is now sometimes dignified by the title, "Evangelistic Music," which is fitting. Without it the Pentecostal Movement could never have made the quick inroads into hearts that it did, nor carried on a constant, victorious revival for fifty years of bringing men closer to God: Nor been ready for the coming of Jesus as many are to-day; accepted, sealed, and shipped through this world in bond, until He appears.

I know some will disagree with me on this subject of music but all the same, it was a practical, old-fashioned, down-to-earth type of singing which all could handle and enjoy, so God used it, as He used a manger in the long ago, contrary to all cultured opinion and pride, then or now.

But millions did know the "joyful sound" of the voice of God, and went on to see signs, wonders and miracles in profusion. He, for whom clouds are but the dust of His feet, walked gently through the earth, calling as of old, "Come, Follow me, and I will make thee fishers of men."

Thousands left their "nets" immediately and followed Him as he went down through the highways and byways where dwelt the lowly in spirit, men who would hear and heed him. Such have reaped down His fields and brought in the harvest, into "garners" which He himself established and sustains.

A young man, R. E. Winsett, was the first publisher who began to write hymns especially for the Pentecostal revival. At first he compiled thin, 25 cent, paper-backed books, inexpensive enough so that everyone could take one of these silent preachers home.

When I went into a new house and saw one of our hymn books, usually on the piano where someone had been using it, I knew that it was a home which would be Pentecostal before long, without any further help from me. Even the titles changed people's ideas of God. Some of the titles were as follows:

*Honey In The Rock*
*I'm Happy With Jesus Alone*
*This World Is Not My Home*
*Swelling In Beulah Land*
*The Old Account Was Settled*

*Come And Dine*
*We'll Be Caught Up To Meet Him*
*Death Hath No Terrors*
*O, The Fire Is Burning*
*The Hallelujah Side*
*Something More Than Gold.*

In compiling his books, Brother Winsett seemed to understand the message with which all our hearts were so full, and therefore selected the particular songs which the Spirit could use.

One of his own compositions, however, called Evening Light seemed to me most characteristic of our revival. Based on Zachariah 14:6, Acts 3:19, Mark 16:17, John 12:35 and Matthew 24:32, it was a clear, trumpet-like call to the entire church of God, and never failed to command attention.

Because it was so used of God to alert everyone to the fact that "books of prophecy" were now being "fulfilled *at last*," it is given verbatim here:

*Christians, awake! See the light has come,*
*Shining in evening as clear as morn;*
*Christians, awake! Christians, awake!*
*Now AWAKE and behold evening light.*
*Refrain*
*The evening light has come,*
*The dark day is past,*
*The clouds now have flown,*
*Books of prophecy fulfilled at last!*

*Time off refreshing has come to all,*
*God is now letting His Spirit fall;*
*Christians, awake! Christians, awake!*
*Now awake and receive latter rain.*

*Spiritual signs followed saints of God,*
*Who in apostolic footsteps trod;*
*Christians, awake! Christians, awake!*
*Wake and see holy light shines for all.*

*Walk in the light as it comes to you,*
*Christians, awake! Christians, awake!*
*O, awake! Or the light soon will pass.*

*Look and behold now the fig leaves green;*
*Nearing the end can be plainly seen;*
*Christians, awake! Christians, awake!*
*Wake and Watch! Soon the Bridegroom*
*will come.*

This song was particularly good, for the refrain ended each verse with "Books of prophecy fulfilled at last: which was then startling and outstanding news to us all.

There were some who had already been preaching along this line, no doubt, but not people who actually believed it enough to be living so expectantly. Many will say, "Well, He didn't come, so what?" God has never sent any great world changes unheralded, unprophecied, or to totally unprepared people. Fifty to one hundred years was always given for public warning and preparation; but an inner circle of whatever henchmen he had in the earth were apprised of every change even before that.

But isn't the word "soon" a misnomer? The answer- not with God. He dwells, in
Time, but in Eternity, where even one hundred years might well be considered nearer our word "immediately" than "soon." That being as it may, it

seems that for some, even "soon" may find many still unprepared.

# Chapter 24

In 1911, I did a great deal of travelling, holding Revivals and Camp Meetings in Arkansas and Texas as well a Tent Meeting in Monroe, Louisiana. In the fall, I attended a great inter-State Camp Meeting at Eureka Springs, Arkansas. Brothers Bell, Opperman and many other leading ministers were present. There also God spoke a great deal to us through prophecy and other gifts. By this time the whole movement in the Central states had swung in line with the "Finished work" teaching, the other issue having faded out.

In the fall of 1911, I was married to Miss Ethel Wright, my present wife. She was a successful minister and was, at the time of our marriage, the pastor of the church at Galena, Kansas. During an interval between town meetings, I wired her and asked her if she could meet me in Eureka Springs that weekend so that we could be married. She came, and we were married there in the double parlors of her hotel, the rooms filled with saints from the Eureka Springs Assembly. That night at church, during the service, the audience called aloud and insisted, until Ethel finally consented to preach for them. I had to leave almost immediately for Texas to conduct another Camp Meeting, assisting Brother Fred Lohman, while Ethel returned to her pastorate in Galena. When this Camp Meeting was over, I went back up to Galena and remained there for a while.

We had not at first thought the details of our marriage relevant to this narrative, but when several who have reviewed the manuscript requested it, we decided to include it just as it happened. God took a hand in training us together for a life's work, just as He did in all else. My wife relates the following:

Throughout my early years I knew little about God except what my mother had taught me. That He had plans, a program, or even a disposition, I had never suspected. Fear and dread of Him ruled my life.

My mother was a lovely Christian character whom I deeply respected and loved. In her teens, however, she had married instead of following her call to the mission field. As my father was what is usually called a "good man," but not fully a Christian, she soon saw her mistake and adjusted to it, but lost her place in God's work.

Being her first-born, I was diligently trained to follow the leading of God, and not my own preferences, especially in marriage.

With God so far away from the earth-as it seemed to me-a great fear formed in my heart that God might happen to untie me to someone whom I might consider ever repulsive, since He knew so little about what went on down here amongst us.

Conviction pressed, so heavily upon me that I finally surrendered to God somewhat, but through love of the world, actually told the Lord I wanted only enough salvation to keep me out of Hell.

Later a boy whom I did not particularly fancy, began proposing marriage to me. Remembering that he was one of the only three Christian young men, I happened to know at the time, I looked to God silently while idly riffling the leaves of a Bible near me. Casually it fell wide open and I read the following startling words. Could it be an answer to such a trivial prayer? But these words stood out, and I knew definitely that for *some reason* God *meant them for me.*

"*What God hath cleansed*"-That must mean saved, I reasoned, "Call *thou not common nor unclean*" which meant that God considered him my equal whether I did or not.

"*Rise, Peter; kill and eat!*"

This I thought likely meant that I was to accept what God was giving me-*If* he really was. Did the Lord really want me to marry this boy for whom I hadn't the least affection? But actually, knowing so little about God, I could not decide.

Left dazed, even speechless, by this appalling idea, I turned without a word and walked blindly out into the woods, alone with God. I was almost wild with fear. What I had been dreading seemed to have come upon me! I knew I had to contact God, even if I must search all Infinity to find Him! I had to know what He really meant!   Three days and nights my soul went questing. I wrestled, implored, and strove to find Him, but to no avail. God, in the meantime, was wrestling with my own pride, my aversions, and high esteem in which I held myself. Once a few words were clearly and distinctly impressed upon my mind, "Whatever made you think you were something special?" That successfully finished deflating my ego-temporarily, at least.

After "dying out" as best I could to ambition, selfishness, worldliness, and pride, yet without suspecting the importance of the overhauling God was giving me, I fell, in Spirit, surrendered and broken before Him.

Then it was that He told me to go open the Bible again, and He would show me the man he had really chosen for me. At the same time a deep, sweet peace crept through my trouble mind and spirit.

By this time, I was so overhauled it didn't matter whom I married. So *My Lord* was *pleased*. The Scripture I opened to first was this:

"And he had a son, a choice young man and a goodly; and there was not among the children of Israel a goodlier person than he; from his shoulder and upwards he was higher than any of the people." (1 Sam. 9:12)

Then one other Scripture which I could not at all understand. This puzzled me greatly. It was Mark 1:3 to 9 which I did not guess inferred that he would be some kind of preacher. But that he would be a preacher-another of my pet aversions-never dawned upon me! From that time on I waited for the man whom God had planned to send me, hoping I would recognize him enough not to refuse his proposal, and so disturb God's planning.

Because of inexperience as a Christian, coupled with a lot of imagination about this promise of God, I was soon off on another fanciful mirage. There gradually began to develop in my mind the image of a creature who was more angel or dream than man.

There were no older brothers in our family from whom I might have concluded that, after all, men were only men. I really pitied "the fallen ones," as I supposed-the prosaic men of my acquaintance. Men, run-of-the-mill men, had never impressed or held much attraction for me, because of their imperfections, their lack of glamour; perhaps mostly their morals, I thought.

After this, I was less impressed than ever. But I was fully convinced that somewhere, there was at least one ideal man. One who was perfect! Absolutely perfect!

Of such strong material was this dream fabric woven that it was many years after I was married before the idea ever entirely percolated through that my husband could be wrong about anything.

At first, he only laughed at such ideas of himself, then later tried seriously to point out my mistake. It was not easy for me to see.

Things finally righted themselves, of course, and I could evaluate life as it really existed. But I'm afraid I still retain that faint impression that "above all the children of Israel"-church people to me-there is not "a godlier person than he." He is still "higher than any of the people," and very "choice" so far as I can see. (And I know a lot of others who would like to shout "Amen" to that!"

My husband, of course, never held with any such naive fantasies about himself, for he is a most realistic person.

Nor was it until one day, long after we were married, when I happened to be studying the first chapter of Mark, that I understood that God in the long ago had not only been showing me the man I was waiting for, but as well, the particular message he would bring.

But from then on I waited for this dream creature, ideal in looks, morals, intelligence, principles and all.

As I could not possibly recognize him until God pointed him out to me, he walked into and lived in our town all unsuspected.

Brother and Sister Goss came-the first to bring the Pentecostal doctrine to our town. After I became Pentecostal, I accepted them as messengers of the Lord, and, as ministers, grew to like and respect them very much. Sister Goss usually asked me to spend the night with her when her husband was traveling and she was alone. Him, I knew little. I can look back now and see that we rarely ever spoke, but I was not conscious of it then, as that was a congregation of several hundred people, and I would have been embarrassed had I attracted attention. I admired his principles, his character, and his courage in his work, but not himself as a man. He seemed too ordinary. So blinded was I by preconception that, if God had not worked, I do not think I could ever have been conscious of him. Brother Bell shortly became my pastor and continued so, until I went out in the work.

After Sister Goss unexpectedly passed on, Brother Goss travelled constantly, and we saw him but little. He was still to me just another married man, and now, what was more remote in my eyes, a widower. I was very prejudiced against widowers; why I do not know.

Then one night while I was engrossed in doing altar work in a crowded tent campaign, God unexpectedly spoke kindly in my ear and said: "Look over your left shoulder and you will see the man you are to marry."

Surprised, even stunned, I remained motionless, but fumbling over in my mind as to who it might be, for I knew that there was no one there whom I myself would have chosen. Heartsick from fear and dread, I decided I would not look. *I did not want to know!*

Subconsciously, I suppose, I was trying to evade God and get out of it. But I really felt, at the moment, like a lamb being unwillingly led to slaughter.

Finally, God settled it for me by sternly speaking one mere word: *"Look"!*

Reluctantly, I obeyed.

Under that entire side of the tent there stood only one man. He was wearing a dark summer suit, and he stood in the midst of an entire section of women in what appeared to be light summer clothing. Bewildered, I saw that it was only "Brother Goss." Again puzzled, perplexed, it did not register. I could not see how he would enter into the picture, unless, happy thought, he might be going to perform the ceremony. "That's it!" I thought triumphantly. "The Lord couldn't have meant *him*;-not for a *husband!*"

"Of course I had misunderstood the Lord," I decided further. It should at least be someone new. Someone romantic! Someone thrilling!

Going on with my altar work, I was soon seized by uneasiness for fear he might happen to walk near me, or accidentally to speak to me while I was so perturbed.

In this confused state of mind, I glanced around to see that all was clear. I slipped out and slowly walked home, talking to God as I went.

By this time I understood Him better. I said; "But, Lord, I don't love that man. If you mean him. I'm disappointed. I've always expected someone quite different."

So for days I thought it over before the Lord, and tried to decide, I watched him on the platform to see what he might really be like, still hoping I was mistaken.

Then I began to wonder if I could possibly follow through with such a plan *if* it became necessary. And, as God hadn't answered my prayer, nor spoken further to me on the subject, I began to suspect that God, after all, had really meant exactly what He had said.

I was deeply disturbed and sad. For days I was only subconsciously aware of what appeared to me to be a delicate, feathery, columnar cloud of pale, softly curling smoke. It began drifting down from the sky straight into my heart.

So gently and unobtrusively it fell that at first I was scarcely conscious it was happening.

As the days went by, this gentle falling gradually increased in velocity. I finally discerned that it was love for "Brother Goss" that God was pouring down into my heart from Heaven.

When He finally made me sure that this was His will for me, I hesitated no longer but gladly surrendered my will to His.

"Lord," I said, "if you are actually performing such a miracle for me, then it is up to me to say 'Thy will be done.'" I had not known before that it was within God's power to do such a thing as this.

I can't tell you how God was able to drastically rearrange my thinking. I only know that soon there dawned upon my horizon a new man, a thrilling new stranger, only five year older than I, handsome, efficient, desirable; and that under God's tutelage my heart was all his. So greatly was this true, that he still seems to have been two different men even yet. From then on my big job was how to hide all this from him, and to appear as unconcerned as I had been before.

This complete thought-change has since shown me how easy it can be for any of us to so *develop our own ideas* that, if left to ourselves, we could gladly die for them, believing in our hearts that we were right, and everyone else wrong.

Does it not point out the fact that often a strange, willful, and unsuspecting that pattern emerges in our lives, perhaps coloring, even dictating, important decisions-decisions which might even change the entire course of a life?

It is possible that some of the foremost religions of the world have in the past been unsuspectingly formed by just such a solidified, crystallized, fully completed thought-pattern.

An old Southern spiritual, recognizing this fact, reasons:

"Somebody wrong about the Bible, I believe-I believe."

Since the Bible has emerged from the ages as the only true standard of all right thinking,
Will it be safe, in the end, to be other than God-directed?

Then wisely my tiny grand-tots sing the little chorus:

"My Lord knows the way through the wilderness.

All I have to do is follow!"

Earlier than this, Howard had a somewhat similar experience.

After his young wife's passing, he had decided in his own mind never to remarry, but to devote himself exclusively to the Lord's work. He loved the Lord and felt that he would like to "go the last mile" in order to please him. But this proved not to be in God's plan for him, although he didn't suspect it at the time.

One day he had been out of town all day. Two of his old friends, leading evangelists, were then beginning to conduct what proved to be a successful revival. When Howard returned in the evening, they immediately invited him to go to the garden with them.

170

"Howard," they said, "we have something very personal to say to you. We hope you will not be offended, but we still feel we should tell you because we believe it to be of the Lord."

"What is it?" he asked.

"Your future wife was at church this morning," they replied. He did not at once comprehend what they meant. Not all impressed, he asked, "My what?"

"Your future wife," they repeated.

Trying to be courteous, he idly asked: "What made you think so?"

The Lord showed each one of us separately during the morning service" (one had been up preaching) "that this particular girl will be your wife. After the service was over, we compared notes, and found that both revelations were exactly the same."

Howard didn't take any stock at all in their words at the time. The only thing it did do, he said, was to set him wondering why they had never imagined such a thing. We were about ready to married if I remember correctly, before I knew of the incident.

I remember the morning well. The new evangelists had arrived on a late-night train the night before. None of us had ever seen them; naturally, we were curious.

The next morning, I was hindered from arriving at the eleven o'clock service on time. However, I was impressed to go anyway, so I approached the big tent at about twelve just as the call of prayer was to be given. I slipped into next to the back seat, but almost immediately the speaker turned to the other evangelist and spoke to him. Then- as far as I could tell- they both looked straight at me and began whispering about me. I was both nonplused and embarrassed, and hoped no one else would notice it. Impatient with what I thought must have been only my own imagination; I began to tell myself how presumptuous it was of me even to think such a thing. I went to prayer asking God to forgive me for such egotistical ideas and tried to forget it. By this time, we had begun to hear from other workers telling us that God had shown the same thing to them, and saying "God bless you."

Some, for other reasons, said antagonistic things, but we soon decided the devil held himself ready, at all times, to cast aspersions on what God had set out to do. But as for me, my heart was satisfied; my dream had come true.

It would occupy too much space to tell how God worked with both of us, revealing His will to us, and to the other ministries as well. He not only revealed His will, but graciously confirmed it every step of the way. A few instances will suffice.

When later we became engaged to be married, we set the time for the following summer. This must be the Lord's will, we reasoned, as it was the first spare time either of us would have, so far as we knew then.

But the Lord cut across our plans and began to deal very definitely with Howard. He telegraphed Galena where I was stationed, asking if I would meet him in Eureka Springs and marry him on Monday.

Since I was never one to make or change plans readily, it didn't occur to me to accept. I prepared to send my regrets.

Wording the telegram, however, became difficult. While praying about it, my hand was stayed. It came to me that in a matter of such importance, in lieu of my mother, I should first confer with Sister Arthur, a much older and more experienced minister who I felt sure would help me arrange the telegram. She had had the overseeing of the Galena Mission ever since she and Howard had come into "Pentecost." She knew the ways of the Lord much better than I.

When, as a preliminary, I read the telegram to her and asked her what she thought I should do, she answered with a happy smile, "Why go!" "Go?" I questioned, astonished. "Yes!" she emphatically answered. Then I explained our previous plans. "Hasn't anyone told you what the Lord showed Sister Coffee?" she asked. Sister Coffee was an evangelist, also a member of the Church. "No," I said, wonderingly.

Then she told me that ten days before in a prayer meeting (which the Lord had directed me definitely not the attend), God had spoken to the Church through Sister Coffee, in prophecy, and had told them all that He was planning for Ethel and Howard to be married soon. I have now forgotten the rest of the message. Sister Miller, the church secretary-treasurer, was immediately shown a vision telling her we were to go to *Eureka Springs* to be married soon. That I was to return as pastor for the following six months.

This was all news to me….The strangest thing was that this was the only way they had of knowing we were *even engaged* as I had told no one; neither had Howard. It later turned out that each member was so sure someone else had already informed me that no one had mentioned it to me.

Sister Arthur said: "Go over and talk to Sister Miller, and see what she says. I've never known her yet to be mistaken in knowing the Lord's voice. She has your expense money ready."

Sure enough, when I walked over and talked to Sister Miller, she handed me my train fare, my hotel expense, and some money for incidentals. This had all been contributed by the members of the Assembly especially for my use. They had found out exactly how much I would need. She also gave me money from the treasury for the telegram.

This happened on Friday morning. I sent the telegram. Sister Arther told me that the one woman who hadn't contributed said she would supply my trousseau. So, I spent Friday afternoon downtown shopping for a trousseau. This was done also without any planning or forethought on my part.

I took my regular Sunday appointments, and left on the midnight train for Eureka Springs. As soon as Howard arrived the next day, he sent an invitation to the Eureka Springs church to be present at three o'clock that afternoon.

Then there was the matter of a wedding bouquet. Money was so scarce in those days that I felt what little we had could be more profitably spent on essentials than on a wedding bouquet. Because of an inherited love for flowers, which seems to be in my blood, this caused me some regret, but I brushed it aside.

Just in time, and most unexpectedly, the lady who owned the hotel came in with quite a few hot-house blossoms for me. I quickly fashioned them into a simple bouquet, which I carried. And, so we were married Monday afternoon in the double parlors of "The Chatangua Hotel" with a large group of saints in attendance. How my heart rejoiced to know so definitely that we were in His precious will and care.

Sister Arthur later said that the Lord had several times whispered to her previous to this prayer meeting of our forthcoming marriage, although she knew of no engagement.

This Assembly was the most quietly efficient group of saints in the Spirit it was ever my privilege to know, and "I thank my God upon every remembrance of them."

They felt we would be so perfectly suited for the Lord's work that they were happy and so were we. Time proved them right.

# Chapter 25

We were sometimes asked why, if God wanted to restore Pentecost to the earth and fill people again as in Apostolic days, He turned to us instead of to the trained ministry who were already recognized as spiritual leaders-albeit some were far from spiritual.

Then I did not know the answer. Now, I think it could have been because ninety percent of us were so very young. When God set thousands of us on fire with a heavenly passion, we balked at nothing. Most of us had no formal training for the ministry, so we had no close, resultant loyalties-all restrictive –such as church fixations, doctrinal prejudices, old college ties, ministerial pride or acquired dignity to uphold. Our loyalty was to Christ alone.

Most of us were merely ordinary, aggressive young people, overwhelmingly in love with Jesus, the "fairest of ten thousands," the altogether lovely One, and we "Loved not our lives unto death." Thus we became selfless, detached. His will became our will. We had no other. No sacrifice was too great, no duty too hard for us to perform. No indignity we could suffer could favorably compare with what Jesus had already suffered for us, and we were grateful. Without wishing to cast aspersions on any person or situation, I would, nevertheless, like to include some naked truths here.

The usual ecclesiastic of that day was not flexible enough for God to use him in a new religious movement on the earth, such as this. It was an end time message, a fulfilling of Joel's prophecy, which God had not idly given in the first place. It was, no doubt, intended to be characteristic of tis entire dispensation from Jesus' day until now. But its fulfillment had all along often been so hampered by doubtful clerical teaching, generally speaking, that God, seemingly had to side-step the organized unit, and raise up a malleable people, in order to "bring to pass his Act, His strange Act," (Isa 28:21) as Isaiah had prophesied.

But the Lord foresaw how successfully the fullness of His purpose in the earth would soon be frustrated and nullified by the uninspired teachings and pronouncements of men, and how even the plain, simply worded teaching of Peter on the day of Pentecost would quickly become equivalent to heresy, and would be abolished, abrogated, expunged.

The first offense by uninspired teachers was that the time period of Acts 2:17 was "put far from thee," relegated to some for distant era, which could not possibly concern them. Then the "Daughters" were forbidden to prophecy; the "hand maidens" were silenced. Young men" were shacked, so checked, so retarded that comparatively few virile, red-blooded young men would endure the oppression for long. Thank God for the few reformers who did! The "dreams" of "old men" were frowned upon and made light of! There was little place for spirituality anywhere outside a tightly closed pulpit, and sometimes very little there.

"Signs and wonders" were said to be fanatical. Miracles were all for past ages, a phenomenon not for everyday use. Physical healing had been for Jesus alone to perform while on the earth. Faith was a dead flame, a candle snuffed out. The true baptism of the Holy Ghost, with the evidence of speaking in other tongues as the Spirit gave utterance at Pentecost, was held to be an experience so far above human reach that only the twelve Apostles were ever qualified to obtain it.

Not even the teaching of the power and happiness of a truly regenerated life was left to bless sorrowing humanity be many denominational preachers. A defeatist religion was proclaimed and believed everywhere. "Just do the best you can, and hope for the best after death" might well have epitomized many pulpit messages.

Think how much precious fruit from the earth God could have had to gladden His soul. Think how many hopeless, doomed, lost men and women down through the ages, now eternally lost, could have been rejoicing in a risen Savior's love, had the "young men" and the "daughters," ever since the resurrection, been allowed to prophesy, to be "led by the Spirit" on their own, and to carry gospel light into Earth's darkest and most remote corners! Had Christians everywhere been receiving the energizing and propelling power inherent in the baptism of the Holy Ghost-had been eagerly witnessing, as they do to-day-what might have been wrought!

But Satan didn't die when Judas hanged himself. He shifted his position a bit, and then went to work on the preachers. May God preserve us!

An eminent pastor, writing in a recent issue of a woman's magazine, gives a fair cross-sectional view of some present-day church-members, and delineates for us a few of the main categories into which they fall. As the picture had changed little with the years, it is still recognizable.

Number one on his list seems to be the selfish type: self-centered people who want nothing of God beside peace of mind for themselves, and to be let alone.

Another is the self-complacent worshipper, "having a form of godliness, but denying the power thereof." This writer says: "Indeed, this kind of churchly respectability can become genuine religions' most deadly enemy"..."they are immune to the real meaning of religious faith"..."Many churches have become so accommodating and easy-going in their requirements...that almost anyone feels at home there."

Then there was also the wholly congealed type, so frozen in their own human goodness and perfections, that they couldn't thaw out. Human nature, even though it may be called to preach, seems to prefer to lead God around, monkey-like, on a string-if it could be done-rather than to be completely emptied of self, and allow God to lead and control themselves.

Still another group offered of contemplation are those "self-opinionated, intolerant folk, who go to church to have their prejudices confirmed."

There are also members of another class who worship their denomination far more than they worship God Himself. The first time I ever heard this statement in words, it was made by a young farm boy who stood up in a testimony service and challenged all church fold to prove him wrong. He said: "You'll let a man who is working with you curse Jesus Christ all day, and never turn a hair; but let him curse or vilify your church even once, and you will immediately knock him down."

Again, some people think of themselves as Christians but say they are "not an emotional Christian." To my way of thinking such a state cannot exist. Love is the most transcendent emotion known to our race. Where love is, emotions are paramount.

Especially where "All the head, mind, soul, and strength" are given over to love, as Jesus commanded, Salvation becomes a surging river of emotion, carrying the Christian triumphantly through whatever may lie ahead.

Of such cordage are martyrs made. No substitute for love has the necessary tensile strength for the everyday stresses and strains of life. Nor will any substitute produce those "who loved not their lives even unto death."

True Christians soon learn that this deep, ceaseless, surging tide of love for Christ creates the only worship worthy of His Holiness. So, he who is truly a Christian cannot, in the very nature of things, escape being emotional, however much atrophied religionists may insist to the contrary. But, as the bird is adjusted to wind and shy, so the Christian lives in this exalted sate of perfect peace, perfect exhilarating rest and tranquility, until, for them, it becomes the norm.

Only by abandonment to Christ's love can the soul come at last into its true habitat-the great loving heart of a magnetic Savior.

However, characteristic of those whom the Lord gathered into the Pentecostal movement were the ones who humbly bowed low before the Savior, smiting the heart, and crying, "God be merciful to me, a sinner."

These truly found Him in earth-shaking power, and went home justified, just as they did in Jesus 'day.

Led by the Spirit, many church ministers however, at great cost to themselves came amongst us, receiving the Holy Ghost baptism in its fullness, afterward successfully leading our customary nomadic life of faith.

Brother E. N. Bell, whom I have mentioned before, was granted a year's leave from his city pastorate in order to go to Brother Durham's Mission in Chicago, where he would 'tarry' and seek God for his portion of this Latter Rain outpouring.

For eleven months this humble scholar placed his mind, his heart, his life at God's disposal, waiting upon Him, unloading ideas which God pointed out were inconsistent, and embracing the viewpoint that God was approving.

By the end of the eleven months he was really made over, a new man, and taught by the Holy Spirit of God. Through this daily process of absorption and assimilation, he became so filled with God that he abundantly overflowed in other tongues.

Because of this precious time spent on his knees studying God, and His Bible, he later became one of the Movements great teachers, and a blessing to thousands.

But not all the men of note who came investigating remained with us. Everyone who was hungry enough for God, and willing to pay God's price, got God's best. People who wanted God at any price were neither captious nor fault-finding, but overlooked, everything they did not understand when they realized God was in our midst, just as we had originally done.

Some preachers, notwithstanding, came to the services, contemptuous of the leaders, curtly polite, hoping to grab off whatever we had that looked like God, appropriate it for themselves to wear as a decoration of honor, solely due their position and their years of ministerial service.

But God was against even the slightest trace of a pharisaical spirit, so they went away empty. They were already too full of self-admiration to be the one hundred percent empty vessel which God unfailingly filled. So young people, sinners, infidels, almost everyone went into the kingdom of God before they did.

Others were not willing to "tarry until." They felt it was too great a waste of their important time, and ignored the fact that one must take time to be "plunged, immersed, steeped and soaked" in the Holy Spirit of God before one could really be Spirit-baptized.

Still others had so much consecrating to do that they became secretly peeved with God and walked away. This type usually later spread detrimental stories against the work to ease their own consciences, and thereby hindered many who might otherwise have gone after God's best. But God rode gloriously on, scattering His bounty where He would, leaving the "elder brother" dazedly standing in the road-so to speak-watching His dust.

Because it was He Himself at work, God dipped down and touched scattered cities, villages and hamlets with celestial fire; and He Himself lighted hundreds of flame-tipped, altar-inspired witnesses of His Power to heal, recreate, and make anew.

Nor did He leave Himself dependent upon someone to go, but skipped over distance, bringing hills and plains and seas to life, throbbing with glory and adulation. Isolated missionaries about their work heard a Heavenly "going in the mulberry trees" and gladly welcomed to One who "stood over by the threshing floor of Arunah," who had also strengthened Gideon. They, too, opened hungry hearts wide to the very "King of Glory," and Heavenly Glory poured in until they literally ran over. "Then were our lips filled with singing" and our hearts with rejoicing!

Signs and wonders and gifts of the Holy Ghost followed all these wherever they went, exactly as He had promised in the dispensation.

Ah, those were glorious days! Days of Heaven upon earth for everyone fortunate enough to have received Him. He is most truly King of Glory-King of the glory-filled heart!

Hundreds of Assemblies sprang up everywhere.

Many others who had been hungry for God were now encouraged to come nigh Him, and to receive Him for themselves. Many who had imagined they were saved now found they had never been truly converted. The gospel was preached to poor and rich alike, the poor coming up and the high coming down, as John had prophesied (Isaiah 40:4).

John was called "a Voice." Some of us can be only echoes, because we lack the "rivers of living water" Jesus promised at the feast (John 7:37). For many years we were called "A John-the-Baptist-movement" because it was God's voice crying in a spiritual wilderness of the restoration of all things "spoken by the prophets."

Besides all the individuals who received the Holy Ghost literally "went everywhere preaching the Word." They sowed beside all waters, aflame with their Heavenly experience, and they "ceased not day and night" in every house where they could enter" to declare the wonderful works of the Lord. Many congregations were formed voluntarily. Many who went as Missionaries, backed by no Board, having no earthly means of support, living by faith alone, laid the foundation for the vast Pentecostal Movement around the earth today.

Degrees, parent church boards, good salaries, and restful holidays are all contributing factors upon which evangelistic ministers might base their hope of success. But no human aid so inflames a locality as a preacher and his congregation on fire with the Holy Ghost.

When God wanted to commission Moses to deliver Israel, He got his attention by setting a bush on fire. Now God attracted people by setting men on fire-men who, like the bush, were not consumed, men who were submerged in the things of God, and able to relate what had happened-men in whom there was no self-consciousness, no pretense, no cultivated mannerisms, no playing to the gallery, no stealing the show. All was done in deep sincerity, in burning earnestness, and in the childlike simplicity of true faith. Binding it all was white-hot brotherly love.

For many years our preachers were far more afraid of compromising a message which they believed to be God than they were of backsliding. Walking in the light of God's revelation was considered the guarantee of unbroken fellowship with God. I feel that it still is, for that matter. Consequently, a preacher, who did dig up some new slant on a Scripture, or get some new revelation to his own heart ever so often; a preacher who did not propagate it, defend it, and if necessary, was not prepared to lay down his life for it, was considered slow, stupid, unspiritual. All of them were more afraid of drifting back into "a form of godliness: or becoming "hide-bound," legalistic, "dead," than they were of open sin, because so few fell into sin, I suppose. At least the possibility seemed remote. Calling a man "a compromiser" killed his ministry far and wide. Because of this, no doubt, many new revelations began to cause confusion.

Then we took one of our first open steps toward organization. Finally, it was unanimously approved at one of our Conferences that every minister who received a new revelation was not to preach or teach it publicly until the next Conference. There he was to submit it to his brethren in open session. If none of his hearers could tear it to pieces scripturally, or "shoot it full of holes," and if it came through still in one piece, all preachers would be at liberty to preach it, if they wished.

For many years this was common practice. Our eyes were so constantly being opened to some new phase of the Word of God, that, when we met each other, noting seemed to be so important a topic of conversation as the Scriptures. A familiar and most absorbing question when preachers met was: "What new revelation have you received?"

It was so often mentioned that, years later, after we had moved to Canada, that my wife and I were both shocked and amused when two of our small sons borrowed our language.

It happened this way. The boys had disappeared with their little wagon after lunch one day. When night fell and they had not returned, we began to wonder. There was little danger there; nevertheless, I started out to search for them. They suddenly appeared from another direction, and their mother told them I had gone in search for them, and chided them for being so late. Joseph, the oldest (he was then about six years of age), drew himself up to his full height and said impressively: "Mother, I said to Alvohn at the foot of the hill: 'Alvohn, I've just had a revelation.'" Upon inquiring, she found that Alvohn had stood stock-still, and attentively had asked: "What it is?" Really serious now as he noticed the darkness that had fast settled around them, Joseph told him: "We are going to get punished when we get home!"

As God gave each man a vision, so each man wrought. Our chief concern was that the job He had given us be well and truly done, for we had found that His work must be compounded together and that, Christ being the chief Cornerstone, our work must be of like quality and endurance. So God used us unsuspectingly to lay as well a Scriptural foundation for His Glory, which God has always honored by fire. For truly God's holy fire still falls everywhere on each person who cheerfully consecrates himself as a sacrificial offering to be consumed by God in His service.

We saw only the work to be done at the moment, and were too occupied with duty and opportunity to plan a future. Anyway, God had so effectively taught us that He led His own work and that we were only laborers doing His bidding that all other planning was left entirely to the Master.

# Chapter 26

It was about this time that Ethel and I began our future work as an evangelistic team by conducting a revival in Galena, and a tent revival for Brother S. D. Kinne in Tallequah, Oklahoma. I shall never forget one incident which took place while we were there.

We entered the tent for a Sunday afternoon service at 2:30p.m. The thermometer was high-around 90 degrees. Soon a wind came up from the northwest, bringing rain. Believe it or not, within a half-hour the temperature had dropped from 90 degrees to below freezing. The rain froze over everything; the landscape looked as though it had been carved in ice. I have never seen such a drastic change in weather since.

After attending another Conference in Houston, we returned to Galena, where Ethel later resigned her pastorate so that we could travel. Our first stop was in Eureka Springs where we attended a Bible School that Brother Daniel Awrey was conducting there.

Daniel Awrey was a world-famous Bible teacher, missionary and traveler. He preached wonderfully for several weeks on Philippians 1:19-"The Supply of the Spirit." He had recently spent forty days on an ocean steamer and had stored up the Word of God and an abundant "supply of the Spirit" for himself. He was a man of cultivation and charm, but in his trips around the world, he used little of the abundant offerings he received for himself. In order to save to give to others, he bought steerage tickets and arranged to forego hotels by sitting up in trains at night. By living austerely, with much fasting, he was able to send thousands of dollars through the years to missionaries who were suffering privations in the field. His messages and example were a great incentive to us; his teachings were both practical and deeply spiritual. A great man, and greatly used of God.

During the summer of 1912, we held several two-week Camp Meetings under my tent-at Eureka Springs, at Siloam Springs, at Essex, Missouri, at Malvern, and the last Camp for the season at Hot Springs in Arkansas.

The last-named Camp Meeting proved to be an exceptionally good one with great crowds attending, and with a great moving of the people toward God. We erected the tent on East Central Avenue, near the State Fair Grounds. We were only scheduled for a ten-day meeting. But the crowds were so great that the superintendent of the street railway system came to see me and urged me to continue the meetings, more on his part, perhaps, than on the part of others because of the revenue accruing to him during an off-season period in this resort city. When he found that the tent was to be sent else-where for another Camp, he offered us the free use of the large Whittington Park Auditorium at the other end of town, if we would continue our services.

We moved out to lovely Whittington Park at the other end of the trolley line. God gave us another big meeting there. Assisting us here were Brother Opperman and several other ministers.

To this Park we brought Sister Woodworth-Etter to conduct the evangelistic services, the preaching and the praying for the sick. The fame of her healings had already spread far and wide, so that great crowds gathered to hear her. Many unusual things took place through her great faith in God. Being that rare type-a true evangelist-she became the means of many souls being saved as well as the means of bringing many others closer to God.

Mrs. Etter was a great warrior. Although seventy-two years of age at that time, she was still an ideal evangelist. She never had "days off" or nights. She never seemed to tire; she could keep preaching night and day, year after year, in top form and with the same results. Nor did she ever seem to waver. Nothing daunted or shook her faith. She faced the Devil boldly, but with the quiet authority of perfect assurance. She never gave him quarter. With a faint smile on her face, her right hand slightly upraised, she would calmly and gladly, I think, have walked into a den of lions for Jesus. No matter how helpless nor in what distressful condition the sick and suffering were, she was almost sure to be the first to touch them. If it were a nauseating case, she was usually the last of the workers to leave.

Nor did her evangelistic fervor ever lag. Things basic and fundamental always happened in every service, for God never failed her during all the months I was associated with her.

She never made any attempt to fake a healing, or to cover up, as some of us lesser mortals might be tempted to do. She was simplicity and honest personified. She was dedicated, and honored by the Savior, as results proved. If she ever had a thought outside God's interests, I never heard of it.

A trained nurse, with over thirty-five years service in her profession behind her, was closely associated with her. We all knew her companion very well. She told us that never before had she seen such a courageous, self-sacrificing spirit in anyone. Besides supporting some twenty dependent relatives, she also supported the workers who travelled with her, and paid them all a salary, we were told. Her husband had been an invalid for years, and allowed no one but her to care for him. She arose at six o'clock every morning to make his breakfast and dress him for the day. Apart from her two meetings each day, all her time was spent with him. She never mentioned it either publicly or privately. Her workers told us in confidence. They related the following amusing incident.

Strangers or sinners coming into her meetings often had God's power fall upon them, usually lightly, so that they trembled slightly; but once, when Mrs. Etter was conducting a great revival campaign in Dallas, Texas, God wrought mighty miracles of healing, salvation, and manifestations of different kinds, until the entire country was greatly stirred.

Arriving late one night into the crowded big tent, there walked three very dignified and impressive middle-aged, apparently successful clergymen in full clerical dress. As there was no seating space left, people sitting on the alter benches gave them their seats and the people sat themselves upon the sawdust-covered ground.

In almost all Mrs. Etter's meetings the power of God was so strong that person after person after person each night would casually tumble off their seats and lie for hours as if dead. Those full of faith usually came out of it receiving the Baptism, or healing or whatever they were hungry for.

These three men sat stiffly upright, their eyes alertly following the slightest move on the platform. When the service got well under way with the power of God as strong as usual, one of the clerics, without any to-do, tumbled into the sawdust and lay motionless. Neither of the other two even glanced toward him, unaware, without doubt, that he had changed his position. Five minutes later, perhaps, the next one fell, and in a few moments the third one also toppled into the sawdust where he, too, lay motionless.

Some small boys soon crawled up from the crowded altar floor and appropriated their seats. But the three clerics remained stretched out, dead to the world. The altar service eventually continued around them, and even over them, but they never perceptibly moved a muscle.

After three or four hours, when the power of God had begun to lift, and the altar service was reaching its conclusion, the three pompous clerics arose almost simultaneously, brushed off every particle of sawdust and sheepishly made their dignified way out the door. As they had not spoken a word, no one knew who they were, nor why they had come.

All hoped they got whatever they came for, and that God gave them a double portion of whatever it was.

Sister Etter did tell us privately that her faith had been tested in many ways since she had begun preaching Divine Healing thirty-six years before, or thereabout.

At one time a cancer appeared on the back of her neck, continuing until it had eaten into her spine. The physician who saw it said it was ready to attack the spinal cord. Her family was expecting her death when God healed her, instantly! Throughout the two years of her affliction she had gone right on with her meetings, preaching day and night.

A great woman! A great evangelist-"faithful unto death"!

Cold weather forced us to close the services in the late fall, but not before a great work had been done and a good Assembly established in Hot Springs.

When we had left the park, I leased the Grand Opera House downtown for a period of six months, and invited Brother Opperman to conduct a Bible School throughout the winter. During February 1912, Ethel and I availed ourselves of the opportunity to visit the work in Milwaukee, Wisconsin, in Chicago and in other Northern points. We returned to Hot Springs in the Spring.

Henceforth we remained in Hot Springs as pastors. This was to be our headquarters for several years. I still travelled some, and helped in the general work whenever there was a need. But from this time on I always used a pastorate as a base.

In December of 1912, our eldest son, Joseph, was born in Hot Springs. Ethel now stayed at home with the church, since she did a great deal of the preaching, and was a great help in the Lord's work generally as well as in our own pastorate.

The next summer, I shipped my tent to Meridian, Mississippi, for the first State Camp of the season. It proved to be a great Camp and much good was accomplished for the message of Pentecost throughout that state. Brother H. G. Rogers was one of the chief speakers, while Brother L. C. Hall, the night evangelist, was in top form and really superb.

The next Camp for which I was responsible that summer was in Galveston, Texas. Brothers Opperman, Roselli, Anderson, Hall and many other leaders were there with us. I met Brother Oliver Fausse for the first time there. This Galveston Camp, however, was not the success that most of the others had been.

Soon, from Hot Springs, we left for Tulsa, Oklahoma, to conduct the State Camp there. W. T. Gaston, who was the pastor of the Tulsa Assembly, had invited us to bring the tent to Tulsa. Brother and Sister Hall were preaching for this Camp also, and God surely did give us a great victory. The city was stirred. Brother Willard Pope, John D. James and others assisted us. Altogether we held five State Camps that summer.

# Chapter 27

For some years now we had had no organization beyond a "gentlemen's agreement" with the understanding for the withdrawing of fellowship from the untrustworthy. There was, however, an association of ministers called "Church of God in Christ" to which a few of us belonged from 1910-1914, mainly for purposes of business.

It was becoming increasingly apparent that something would have to be done, if we were to preserve the work. New situations were arising all the time, as our work grew larger and more unwieldy. New attitudes were needed.

In the past we had been taught: "Walk in the Spirit, and ye shall not fulfill the lusts of the flesh." When Brother Canada took charge of the field in 1908, there had seemed to be no need of earthly organization, so none was supplied.

As our numbers increased, the influx brought with it leaders who did not believe in organization at all; some even preached that anything of that nature (when committed to paper) was of the devil. Opposing this viewpoint was the definite system existing in the New Testament church under the Apostles.

As we were all inexperienced, we were carefully testing every step, lest we somehow lose our precious fellowship with God. We were not yet too sure of our ground. Walking in the spirit was all right for those who would, and did, but what of those who wouldn't? What of those who needed more restraint to do their best work?

Carefully and prayerfully watching the work over the years, I hoped to arrive at a decisive conclusion as to what was God's will for *us,* as I had no desire to grieve or to displease the Lord.

It was obvious that men who would voluntarily go into a new, field, who would fulfill the requisite obligations of fasting, praying, preaching, visiting and singing; who would suffer the privations and hardships entailed, and who would give up their own lives to rescue lost souls and mold them into another well-established, frontier life-saving unit, able to rescue others in turn; -to repeat, it was obvious that such men truly loved their flocks, and would lay down their lives for them if the need arose.

Neither could such men take their responsibilities lightly, but were true fathers to these infant Assemblies in every sense of the word. They could pastor a church for years without bringing a reproach to it. These were trustworthy men, men of sound judgment and character, men who were thoroughly saved from both self and sin, having themselves well in hand, under God

Such a man soon associated himself with other preachers who were like-minded. He decided what doctrine he himself believed, had his own fixed standards of right or wrong by which he judged men, knew what conduct he required of his friends, and, in short, carried his own private organization in his head.

I saw this happen over and over again. It worked in the same way on the foreign Mission field. And in new states. Wrong practices brought disapproval from better men. Thus every man, of necessity, had his own unwritten organization, his own unwritten manual, but a manual and an organization nevertheless

Younger ministers, appraising the older ones, naturally grouped themselves around the more fatherly type of ministers looking to him for counsel, example, and fellowship. These groups grew in ever-widening circles, until we really had an unwritten organization, with each group functioning separately, however much we had tried to avoid it.

Unelected officials were produced in the same way. Men naturally gravitate toward the work they like best. Their gifts, whether natural or spiritual-often both-were soon known. Leaders instinctively turned to the one best fitted for the job.

Men among us, in this way, became a secretary, a treasurer, or a leader, not by "usurping" the place, as was sometimes suggested, nor by self-appointment, as was sometimes charged. They were chosen because they were capable and the general public had confidence in them.

A leader also carried in his mind a list of each man's qualities and experience, and thus was immediately able to suggest a suitable person for any appointment.

For instance, it was sometimes difficult to find a suitable local man so well known in a community for his integrity that the public mind would be at rest when he was asked to serve as, say, a Camp Meeting treasurer or official. There had previously been much accusation of corruption in some of the older churches along financial and moral lines, so much so that, whether true or untrue, the lack of confidence had to be lived down before the Pentecostal Movement could be entirely trusted.

It also seemed to me that God, in creating human beings, had naturally conditioned them to fit into working groups after the family idea, and that for this there was no alternative except to become out-and-out outlaws, with eventually "every man's hand…against his brother."

This was contrary to the Spirit of Christ in most of us. Neither did that seem to be God's plan. None of us had any wish for a "hide-bound" organization, the usual term for any degree of ecclesiasticism, for all of us wanted to be free, but so far, there seemed no satisfactory substitute.

Another unhealthy problem was that the Movement, as it grew, began not only to solidify into small clusters around a favorite leader, but often to develop a partisan spirit as well! So much so that each group unconsciously, even copied its own leaders' mannerisms, even as they copied his life. Looking over a Camp Meeting or Convention audience, you could soon spot the followers of the various leaders. Some might yell a quick "Amen" in a happy falsetto like Brother Pinson. Another might jerk his head a little to one side as Brother Durham did when the touch of God came upon him. Or some might have still more noticeable manifestations, if their leader happened to be of the spectacular type.

This growing likeness was easily traced back to the early days of the open West, as I remember it, when groups of law-abiding citizens were forced to band together to weed out the bad men and protect the good.

It was obvious that we were almost following the primitive pattern of the wild Western mustangs which had once roamed the prairies. These creatures grouped themselves into many small bands, each following their own leader, but fighting every other leader and his band as well.

This primeval state of things had never served the best interests of civilization; neither was our system now serving the best interests of the kingdom of God.

The cohesiveness, which God had given us in the Baptism of the Holy Ghost through love was rapidly being lost through our lack of co-operation, and the spirit then abroad in the land which was endeavoring to separate us.

But to the public, this partisan spirit could not be justified, or explained. An Assembly could understand why an irresponsible minister could not be fellowshipped, -why some of his ideas had to be preached against, -but not why good men would break fellowship or split hairs over some minor point of doctrine, practice, or belief, such as now threatened us.

The truth was that if a preacher's spiritual and mental pride was small, he could bear with and work with others who could not honestly see eye to eye with him on all points. If his pride were great, fellowship for him-and with him-was impossible.

Again, varied enterprises, home and foreign missions, for instance, required some sort of organization. These would prosper more if a concerted effort were made, and a stronger home base established.

Within their own consciousness leaders themselves began to recognize gifts and qualities from God in other leaders, far exceeding their own along certain lines. Such men were sent for, their judgment deferred to, much as a pastor secures an evangelist because of his confidence in the other's ability to do the work of an evangelist.

In this way, and in no other, as far as I know, several ministers who scattered over the States and Canada eventually became leaders of leaders. Not by effort or pushing, not by self-praise or electioneering, but because men everywhere had found that the word of wisdom was in them. Or perhaps the prayer of faith, or teaching, evangelism, or some other of the Spirit's gifts. Men made way for them and pushed them up to the top, whether they wanted a top place or not. In this way we also had our unelected officials. Water will find its level and so will men, and "a man's gifts make room for him."

Many regrettable things began taking place at this time in our Southern work, but things so subtle and elusive as to defy remedying.

As our ministers had no written credentials, they casually walked into a church for a meeting whenever they felt the impulse. The churches became so accustomed to it that they heartily welcomed anyone who claimed to be a Pentecostal preacher.

However, up until this time our work had been known by the name "Apostolic Faith". But as these and some other reproaches had been and were being brought upon us, we decided to call ourselves "Pentecostal". The baffling tales abroad, reproached us in the eyes of many people before we could even get a hearing. If they heard us, and *then* rejected us, all right. But we did not feel that we should let God's work lie under undeserved reproach if we could evade it. Hence the change.

How this victimizing system got into operation, we never knew, but we soon began hearing from scattered, unpastored churches that they had been invaded by the cleverest of confidence men, posing as our preachers.
As these men were, of course, clever talkers, many congregations never doubted them. They all sensed that they were different, but in what way they didn't know – at least, not in time to save themselves from being "fleeced".
How these crooks found out that we were "sitting ducks" for their evil schemes, we never knew. But we soon knew they were up to no good. Nevertheless, our hands were tied because we had an entire congregation to convince, after we had satisfied our own minds.

The more spiritual members usually observed it, but a leader could not honorably accuse a man publicly, with no evidence but this own suspicion in hand.
When the incident I am about to relate - the last of several – occurred in Hot Springs, Arkansas, I accepted the pastorate at the invitation of the small Assembly, and moved my family permanently.
This city seemed to have become a favorite stopping place for all these derelicts. Hot Springs was a government health resort for venereal and other crippling diseases, and on the main line of the Iron Mountain railroad. The traffic in imposters got so heavy here that the Assembly sent for help.

200

One afternoon two stranger's arrived at the worker's house – not the first by any means, but undoubtedly the worst – dressed exactly as most of our ministers did. They said they were "Apostolic" preachers and were going to attend the service that night. They told which Assembly they had come from and what wonderful meetings they always had. They were invited to attend the seven o'clock street meeting, and then to preach later at the Mission Hall.

The street corner which the city had assigned to our group lay along the main street which ran through a narrow pass formed by two mountains, and which contained the very heart of the business and promenade section.

That night the two men testified and did fairly well, until the last one, trying to impress their hearers with how much power they had, pointed to a telephone pole and said, "By this power I have I can climb that pole unaided," and proceeded to try. Of course, the workers were horrified, and started a song to cover up.

Two policemen who often stopped and listened to the services had come up behind the large crowd, and had stopped in the shadow of a tall building, unseen by these speakers.

They were alerted immediately. One went back to the Station House, only a few steps away, to refresh his memory. Just as the meeting was being dismissed, the two stepped out, arrested and handcuffed our "preachers" for horse-stealing in an Eastern state.

However, this was the most disastrous occurrence I remember. Fortunately, the city being filled with strangers – 200,000 each season – it didn't do too much harm.

These pastorless flocks were usually understood to be under the supervision of some well - known minister, but often not. A church waited and held their own services until the Lord sent someone along to preach for them. No one was ever "called" to a church by vote.

Sometimes a minister was invited. Most often he simply walked in and started preaching. He could stay as long as he liked, leave when the Spirit bade him go, and nothing was thought of it.

When they made their past wrongs right, a few who were lacking in character were accepted among us, for God was giving everyone a chance. Regrettably, these soon failed, and dropped away into private sins. Greed for "filthy lucre" soon followed. Or sometimes these caused trouble.

When they grew bolder and more hardened, some of these would stop over for a few days in an Assembly and usually, with careful boasting, relate to the congregation how many people had been healed, saved or baptized under their ministry, giving the impression – with great modesty – that they were the "great ones."

But God kept His true ministers free from this spirit of covetousness, from love of praise, unscrupulousness and from self-pity by sending them wherever He chose, "without money and without price." These were the ones who had to follow up the wreckage left in the wake of the ministers just mentioned, and in poverty and privations themselves, suffer for the other's greediness, while they helped the Assembly, restored their confidence and encouraged them spiritually.

No man who was really in touch with God ever thought of either going or staying because of finances. Evangelists usually built up a new field through much suffering, then left it, knowing that the next preacher who came along would reap a bountiful financial harvest.

Nevertheless, the church Board or the pastor, if they had one, usually gave the visiting preachers or evangelists all they could afford.

We had almost no systematic defense against these marauders. Individuals who were willing, under God, to be "helpers," had by sheer character and force of their own personality to stand alone and guard the sheep gate from them.

Another trouble was that a leader could guard only so many sheep at a time. What protection did isolated fields which had no shepherd have when some unworthy person, drawn by the scent of gold, invaded their habitation?

Ironically enough, some of these "fleeced" saints would be so hurt that, instead of reasoning that the one that had tricked them was a crook, they would often turn against all Pentecostal people, classing them all as false, and withdrawing entirely from our ranks.

My work often necessitated that I go wherever there was trouble, help the one in charge to quiet the sheep, arbitrate if necessary, and assist in restoring the congregation's confidence in God and in their leader again. This God always helped me to accomplish. But the damage, nevertheless, was becoming great.

With the congregations it was much the same. A member who had a wrong attitude could go from one church to another and might even be received by the new pastor with open arms, no matter how much he had misconducted himself in his former church. Some pastors were tempted to harbor or protect troublemakers because this man's family, his presence, or his offerings made a good showing. And perhaps he could indulge himself in a small bit of personal gloating that, as an up and coming pastor, he had added to his congregation a person intelligent enough to appreciate his superiority, and thus pay it tribute.

Such a one really should have been reproved and sent back home to make his wrongs right. But surprisingly few free-lance pastors saw the importance, or the necessity for doing so.

So I concluded that in church work, as in all else, men of honor naturally flowed together to stand against all forms of wrong, whether from neglect, or through the gamut of self-indulgence, greed, dishonor, and on to outright sin. Ministers who – thoughtlessly or otherwise – were at heart unfaithful, cared little for the morale of the Savior's flock.

Thus from the Acts of the Apostles and our own experiences, I was led to see that Sprit-filled people needed some restraint, just as a horse needs a harness to produce every man helped his brother, and only those who would do so, should be allowed in, was imperative, and God's form for us, as well.

"Not slothful in business" was another Bible command still in force. But it would be necessary for us to conduct our business in the way our present time demanded; and for this, co-operation was needed.

How a man adjusts individually to organization depends largely upon his own viewpoint. If he has the disposition to make a mountain out of a mole-hill, it can be easily done over organization. The viewpoint is all.

Communists think of us a "capitalist slaves." We think of ourselves as the freest people in the world. To us, our laws are a protecting friend. To other minds, those same laws may be a glowering menace.

Someone wrote my wife not long ago and said: "How happy you must be to be free again." Although she did not know to what the writer referred, she smiled and said: "If they only knew, I have never been anything but free."

Laws, being for the lawless, are a protection to men of good will. They rejoice in the safety of which may seem to another to be the bitterest bondage.

The unsaved think the Christian bound. The Christian knows he is as free as a bird circling the blue.

Pentecostal organizations have, as far as I now, been kept loosely controlled enough to protect both infant and mature saints; but the fence is also high enough, the gate "strait" enough, to bar any who may wish to live in a Scriptural danger zone. Some churches, perhaps, are more restrictive than others.

It is all too possible to allow an outlaw spirit to rule one's self, or a church, and so drive ourselves away from the legitimate protection of organization which God established for the good of His own people.

On the other hand, danger will loom in any organization when the leaders, because of the lack of qualified men, must substitute those of little judgment, with no sense of fair play; men self-willed, egotistic, or power-drunk on the little authority vested in them.

Such men can be mean, stingy, or small, as can be found in any cross-section of humanity, if they neglect to pray through their littleness into the bigness of the self-sacrificing Christ.

Had love for others been in their hearts, love would have taught them. Love is one of the greatest unrecognized teachers on earth. It can reduce even the wildest humanity to gentleness; it is a potent civilizing influence to everyone. Love never fails to teach, to uplift, to humanize and to bring the Deity closer to the human heart.

In one way, nevertheless, organization was forced upon us; the attitude church leaders took made the difference. Many whom God had filled might have preferred to go back to their former connections after the revival had not God allowed such leaders to criticize, ostracize, castigate or insult His children, demanding that they traitorously repudiate all that God had done. Others God Himself dealt with personally, and caused them not to return.

In some parts of the country where persecution was not so intense, some of them still retained their membership, although attending Pentecostal services, and were still in good standing many years later.

None, I think, ever really wanted us to set up a separate organization, unless it became imperative. But seeing the bitterness of most church leaders we soon knew that such a course was now imperative.

Perhaps, it is also inevitable that our Movement will crystallize as it grows older and larger, and that it will not escape the vices which vast machinery and power have unwittingly fostered in older denominations. But may the dear Lord come before this materializes!

# Chapter 28

As there was no apparent way to gather up the reins of the different cliques which each seemed in danger of galloping off in its own direction, Brother Bell and I worked privately together on some kind of solution. We later found that Brother Opperman saw this need, too, as did a few other leaders.

We realize that great care was needed at this stage, as we had been strictly taught against *any* form of organization. Irresponsible brethren, if they heard too much, might immediately use the opportunity to poison the saints against us before we could explain, and call us "compromisers!" –a serious charge in those days.

Of necessity, we secretly discussed calling a Conference to organize the work. So, in November of 1913, Brother Bell and I ventured to announce a Conference at Hot Springs, Arkansas, from April 2 to 12, 1914. We signed the original call ourselves.

I say "ventured" advisedly, because we knew that we were likely facing serious opposition, unless God worked mightily. But other leaders took their stand with us, and added their names to the call, which was being published month by month in *The Word and Witness*. I don't think any of us had many rigid ideas as to how all this should be worked out, but we all supported "system" against the threatened chaos of the moment. Among other leaders there still seemed to be apprehension as to our purpose. In spite of all, we stuck to our guns and prayed. This took courage, but it seemed we had a special filling of grace from the Lord, and we truly felt that He was leading.

Most of that winter my family and I spent in traveling. Before we left I had leased the "Grand Opera House" for six months, and had moved our congregation into it.

Brother Opperman conducted a Bible School until April 2.

We went north that winter and visited many different churches on the way, and finally spent several weeks in a revival with Brother Cyrus Fockler in Milwaukee, Wisconsin, where we were royally entertained.

Back home in Hot Springs, we found everything in fine shape with Brother Opperman, who had been perhaps the first one to join us in the call. He had everything in readiness for the Convention and was full of faith that God would work out things for His glory.

A great number of ministers from all over the states arrived to attend this Assemblage. Some came hoping to block us. Others came to back us up. None of us could unerringly reach each other's hearts or minds. So the first few days of prayer, praise and worship were days of tension and suspicion. No one seemed to want to express his ideas first. Sometimes old friends were even ignored for fear of being seen talking to a "compromiser." Many wonderful sermons were preached under the direction of God. Those sermons accomplished the purpose for which they had been inspired by God.

One night a group of opposition ministers met privately and formed a resolution to be brought to the floor-a resolution which they hoped would forestall any move on our part toward rigid organization.

Some of them knew that we wanted to incorporate with rules and regulations and this knowledge, perhaps, had aroused their suspicion.

The next day they unexpectedly read their proposal from the floor. This was a surprise to us, but as we listened, we heard to our great joy our own ideas being read out. The proposal they read is now part of the preamble of the Assembly of God.

Brother Bell has been chosen chairman; I was acting as secretary. He leaned across to me and whispered, "Brother Goss, they have the very thing we need-and want!" I joyfully agreed.

After a lengthy discussion, this resolution passed the Conference unanimously. Then the incorporation resolution was brought on the floor, and after a prolonged discussion, which became a veritably tussle, this, too, was carried.

Then it seemed that Heaven had opened. The power of God fell mightily upon us all. What a glorious time we had rejoicing and worshipping the Lord!

When this thanksgiving had subsided a little, the Lord spoke to us through prophecy, commending us for this move. Thus a long period of strain for Brother Bell, myself, and others was happily ended.

The smile of God seemed to be upon this union of many segments. Whatever adjustments were needed were quickly, easily, and sweetly settled to everyone's satisfaction. When those among us, who had doubted that the Conference would work out satisfactorily, saw how easily God had carried us past the shoals and hidden snags, they felt a mounting confidence in God and decided to co-operate. I think that what we Pentecostal people want to know, anyway, is that God is in any undertaking, and if He is, we are satisfied.

This was the first successful major effort within our ranks to form a general organization. The ideas seemed to catch fire and to spread rapidly. Hundreds, even thousands, came under its influence, and recognized it as a move of God.

The Old Testament Church in the wilderness had possessed a severely strict and closely knit organization under Moses, despite its being deeply spiritual as well.

This church was ushered in with manifestations of God's power, with signs, wonders and miracles, with clouds of fire, columns of smoke, and with God talking and personally leading His own.

The same thing happened again at Pentecost. In the 15th Chapter of Acts, we read that the great Council at Jerusalem passed four decrees of fundamentals, and wrote them down for posterity. The first result mentioned was the cementing of the strained relationship between the church at Antioch and the Jerusalem Church. These were harmonized, and the friction was removed so that all the churches were established in the faith, and increased in numbers daily.

Soon Brother Bell and I incorporated the work in Arkansas, where we were still stationed-he in Malvern, and I in Hot Springs. Later the Corporation was moved to St. Louis, Missouri, and the Headquarters office was established there.

So ends this history with the equitable conclusion of one of the most formidable questions which ever troubled our ranks in those early Pentecostal days. Other men will, no doubt, trace for the world the further development of this church as it is today.

But now the churches had rest, and the peace of God seemed to brood over all. Since that time, the Pentecostal work has grown rapidly so that it has spread all over the earth, and has divided into many large main hives of busy workers, each carrying on orderly, successful work for the Lord.

And God is still working, too. Many have received the different gifts in their fullness, and are sowing Gospel seed and reaping a mighty harvest beside all waters.

And in all great revivals, God did perhaps more than nine-tenths of the work, humanly speaking. Now I can see that He had truly undertaken to get people ready-sealed in bond-for this atomic age and for His coming-His personal appearance as King at Jerusalem.

Thank God that He ever allowed me to come into "His banqueting house" instead of my having wasted my life on the world and its follies as I might have easily done. What a joy it has been to watch God work...to see Him busy in the earth...to see Him establishing His Kingdom in the hearts of men everywhere-even at this very moment!

As for me, I could wish no greater honor than to hear Him say to me: "Well done, good and faithful servant! Enter thou into the joys of thy Lord!"

I only hope I'll merit such recognition when He comes.

The dawn of a new day sheds its beams over the Church of God. The mighty Christ, even Jesus of Nazareth, will soon burst upon this astonished world- "With the voice of the archangel and the triumph of God!"

When the kingdoms of this world have become the kingdoms of our Lord and His Christ, He shall reign forever and ever!

Your Church-bride has put on her glorious garments an awaits you!

Even so, come quickly, Lord Jesus!